1 - ∞

An
Oakham Overture
to
Poetry

Frontispiece
Near Ridlington. A typical lane leading into the heart of Rutland.

"Before the Roman came to Rye or out to Severn strode
The rolling English drunkard made the rolling English road."
G. K. Chesterton p.79

An

OAKHAM OVERTURE

to Poetry

by John Buchanan
(Headmaster, Oakham School, 1958–77)

SYCAMORE PRESS

An Oakham Overture to Poetry
Copyright © John Buchanan 1985 and the
Copyright holders listed on page vi

Sycamore Press Ltd
Wymondham, Melton Mowbray
Leicestershire

ISBN 0 905837 17 7

Photographs by Trevor Hickman
Design consultant Sue Steel
Text set in Japan by
東京印書館
Display typesetting by Parker Typesetting Service, Leicester
Process Planit Litho
Printed by Nene Litho, Irthlingborough
Bound by Woolnoughs of Wellingborough

CONTENTS

I am indebted to the following copyright holders for permission to reprint certain poems and extracts, namely:

1 Edward Arnold (publishers) Ltd. for extracts from *The Practical Criticism of Poetry* by C. B. Cox and A. E. Dyson.
2 Sir John Betjeman and John Murray (publishers) for extracts from *Collected Poems* and *Summoned by Bells*.
3 Chatton and Windus Ltd. and P. Yates for *Smelling the End of Green July* by P. Yates.
4 Constable Publishers for an extract from *The Stricken Deer* by Lord David Cecil.
5 Curtis Brown Group Ltd., London, acting on behalf of the Estate of Ogden Nash for *England Expects* by Ogden Nash; and to the same group, acting on behalf of the Estate of Victoria Sackville-West, for an extract from *The Land* by Victoria Sackville-West.
6 The Executors of the W. H. Davies Estate and Jonathan Cape Ltd. for *Leisure* from *The Complete Poems of W. H. Davies*.
7 The Executors of the C. Day Lewis Estate and Jonathan Cape Ltd. for *Walking Away* from *The Gate*.
8 Gerald Duckworth and Co. Ltd. for *Tarentella* and extracts from *In Praise of Wine* by Hilaire Belloc.
9 Faber and Faber Publishers for an extract from *Four Quartets* by T. S. Eliot; for *Night Mail* from *Collected Poems* by W. H. Auden; for *Six Young Men* from *The Hawk in the Rain* by Ted Hughes; for *Sunday Morning*, *Bagpipe Music* and *Explorations* from the *Collected Poems of Louis Macneice*, and for *The Landscape Near an Aerodrome*, from *Collected Poems* by Stephen Spender.
10 Harcourt Brace Jovanovich for *Portrait of a Machine*, copyright 1923, by Louis Untermeyer, reprinted from his volume *Long Feud* by permission of the publisher Harcourt Brace Jovanovich Inc., and renewed 1951 by Louis Untermeyer.
11 A. D. Peters and Co. Ltd. and The Bodley Head for *Forefathers* by Edmund Blunden.
12 Laurence Pollinger Ltd. and the Estate of Freida Lawrence Ravagate for *Last Lesson of the Afternoon* and *Nottingham's New University* by D. H. Lawrence.
13 Henry Reed and Jonathan Cape Ltd. for *Naming of Parts* from *A Map of Verona*.
14 The Estate of W. R. Rodgers, 1971, and by permission of Lucy Rodgers Cohen, for *Stormy Day* by W. R. Rodgers.
15 G. T. Sassoon for *Base Details*, *The Death Bed*, *The General*, and *Everyone Sang* by Siegfried Sassoon.
16 The Society of Authors as the literary representatives of the Estate of A. E. Housman for extracts from *The Name and Nature of Poetry* and for five poems from *The Collected Works*; and to the same society, as representing the literary Trustees of Walter De La Mare for *All That's Past*, *The Holly*, and *Farewell* by Walter De La Mare; and to the same society, as literary representative of the Estate of John Masefield, for extracts from *The Everlasting Mercy* by John Masefield.
17 A. P. Watt Ltd. and The National Trust, and Macmillian London Ltd., for *If*, *Cities and Thrones and Powers* and *The Mary Gloster* by Rudyard Kipling; A. P. Watt Ltd. and the National Trust, and Methuen London Ltd. for *Danny Deever* by Rudyard Kipling; A. P. Watt Ltd. and the Estate of the late G. K. Chesterton for *The Rolling English Road* and *The Good Rich Man* by G. K. Chesterton.
18 The Hon. Nigel Nicolson for extracts from *Tennyson* by Sir Harold Nicolson.
19 David Higham Associates Ltd. for *Timothy Winters* by Charles Causley.
20 The Marvell Press for *Church Going*, *Poetry of Departures*, *At Grass* and *Lines on a Young Lady's Photograph Album* by Philip Larkin.

PREFACE

This anthology is partly prompted and inspired by two other memorable anthologies. The first, *The Ages of Man*, was published in 1939, and was compiled by George Rylands, my former ADC producer at Cambridge. Despite the outbreak of World War II the work at once established itself as a unique companion to Shakespeare studies. By subtle juxtapositioning of his extracts to illustrate a general theme, Rylands threw a luminous searchlight on each passage so that the most hackneyed quotation acquired new meaning whilst a disregarded passage often gained fresh significance. Rylands chose, in his own words, "to group loosely together those passages which give utterance to the same or similar passions, which express associated ideas . . . which sum up different attitudes to the common problems of daily life . . . or which reveal affinities of style. From time to time one quotation serves as gloss upon another." In so far as this anthology employs a "variations on a theme" approach, it is directly indebted to George Rylands.

The second anthology is Lord Wavell's *Other Men's Flowers*, which was published five years after *The Ages of Man*, in 1944, and towards the end of a war in which Wavell had found himself experiencing the heights and depths of responsibility as the supreme commander of the British forces in Africa and Greece. At the time *Other Men's Flowers* was published, Wavell was Viceroy of India, and it is an astonishing commentary on his character that, despite all the burdens of high office and the emotional aftermath of his war campaigns, he could yet have found time to produce such a work. It is even more remarkable that the binding thread, as he explained in his modest preface, was nothing more than his memory. "Horatius . . . was the earliest poem I got by heart as a small boy. Admiring aunts used to give me three pence for reciting it from beginning to end; a wiser uncle gave me sixpence for a promise to do nothing of the kind. A little later, *Morning Lines* at Winchester laid a foundation on which my memory ever since has been building and furnishing. . . . I have read much poetry and since viii

I had once a very retentive memory for verse, much has remained in my head. . . . It amused me lately to set down in a notebook the poems I could repeat entire or in great part. I have now collected and arranged the poems I set down. . . . I cannot claim that I can now repeat by heart all the poems in this anthology. I think I can safely claim that I once could." There followed a remarkable book of four hundred pages and some two hundred and thirty extracts ranging from *The Rime of the Ancient Mariner* in its entirety to two line epigrams. There was, inevitably, much poetry which could be easily declaimed, Browning, Chesterton, and Kipling being especially represented, and, accompanying many of the extracts, were personal notes by Wavell himself.

This anthology follows humbly after Wavell's in being principally composed of poetry and verse which at one time or another I have myself declaimed or got by heart. Frequently, as former Sherborne or Oakham scholars will know only too well, this has happened in the classroom and if any old pupil of mine chances to acquire this book he (or she!) may smilingly recognise passages in which he was compulsively involved in years gone by. For, with Wavell and G. M. Hopkins, I hold that it is a function of poetry to be declaimed, poetry in its ballad origins being a declamatory art form. Although I would not go so far as Wavell in claiming that one can never properly appreciate a poem until one has got it by heart, I make no apology for having, over a period of thirty years, required numerous pupils to acquire at least a modicum of poetry in this way; I do not believe it will have destroyed their love of poetry and there is even some chance that it may have kindled it.

I have also followed Wavell in providing a commentary on a number of the extracts. Indeed, this commentary, which is essentially derived from classroom experience, constitutes the only valid excuse for producing yet another school poetry anthology. For whilst Wavell could reasonably expect the common reader to be fascinated by his personal selection of poetry, no run-of-the-mill Headmaster could hope to arouse a similar inherent interest, and this anthology must necessarily stand or fall on its possible classroom use. It is my hope that the commentary will provoke discussion and, taken together with the "variations on a theme" poem-order, will sometimes suggest to the teacher a new approach to a well-worn theme.

To this end also a few poems are followed by questions. Essentially these questions are intended to help the pupil towards a better understanding and appreciation of a poem. Clearly much critical analysis will take place in class at the teacher's instigation and of course the teacher will have his own methods of approach to any poem. But on occasions he may wish to leave the reader to himself over a "prep," for example, and it is my hope that at such times the questions may prove to be of some help to a pupil who is in the process of acquiring for himself the skills of literary appreciation. In this connection, although I have tried to avoid the use of unnecessary technical jargon, there are a few essential terms which the reader will need to understand if he is left to study the anthology on his own; these terms are summarised on pages 221 to 223.

The preparation of this anthology has reminded me of my debt to the poets who have so greatly enriched my life, and my natural reaction as a teacher is to try to pass on some of my poetic experience to others. "Those who can, do: those who can't, teach." Inevitably my enjoyment of poetry is restricted by my own limitations of intellectual and aesthetic sensitivity, and any reader of this anthology may well criticise it as appealing more to the pupil's poetic LCM than to his HCF. To this I can only reply that class experience convinces me that, unless their initial introduction to poetry is relevant and comprehensible, the vast majority of pupils will leave school largely unaware of the poetic experience. As in an opera, so with poetry; the theme tunes need to be set sounding in the minds of the audience so that they are recognised with pleasure when they recur in the opera itself. Because this anthology represents my attempts over the years in an Oakham classroom to provide a preliminary statement of this sort on poetry's behalf, I have ventured to entitle it *An Oakham Overture to Poetry*.

To the "onlie begetter"
of this ensuing work

JOHN M. JERWOOD

"all happinesse and that eternitie
promised by our ever-living poet"

I

Poet's Workshop:

Words

T. S. ELIOT
Extract from *Four Quartets, East Coker, V*

So here I am, in the middle way, having had twenty years—
Twenty years largely wasted, the years of *l'entre deux
   guerres*—
Trying to learn to use words, and every attempt
Is a wholly new start, and a different kind of failure
Because one has only learnt to get the better of words
For the thing one no longer has to say, or the way in which
One is no longer disposed to say it. And so each venture
Is a new beginning, a raid on the inarticulate
With shabby equipment always deteriorating
In the general mess of imprecision of feeling,
Undisciplined squads of emotion. And what there is to
   conquer
By strength and submission, has already been discovered
Once or twice, or several times, by men whom one cannot
   hope
To emulate—but there is no competition—
There is only the fight to recover what has been lost
And found and lost again and again: and now, under
   conditions
That seem unpropitious. But perhaps neither gain nor loss.
For us, there is only the trying. The rest is not our
   business.

"One of the unhappy necessities of human experience," Eliot once wrote, "is that we have to find things out for ourselves," and these lines are an attempt to convey the poet's creative problems. Not only is the contemporary writer faced with the achievements of mighty predecessors who have already scaled their particular Everests but the writer's raw material of language has been cheapened and debauched by slack and extravagant use. In the *Four*

Quartets Eliot makes his finest poetic attempt to understand the movement and meaning of time, and these lines describe something of his struggle to capture what is equally elusive, truth and beauty in poetic form. Even at the very moment when the poet feels he has captured in words precisely what he is straining to express, even at that moment there is a sense of failure and he is back where he started.

Eliot's colloquial vocabulary and superficially casual, even dead-pan, tone, conceal great subtleties of rhythm—the line enjambement seems to match the flickering thought—and the phrase "the years of *l'entre deux guerres*" not only typifies the brilliant use which Eliot habitually makes of compressed allusion but leads into a sustained metaphor of warfare which effectively summarises his poetic struggles.

The passage raises several interesting discussion points. What does Eliot mean by there being "no competition?" Is there, in fact, no building on tradition or the work of others? What is it that he sees as being "lost and found and lost again and again?" Are conditions today in fact so "unpropitious" for the poet? Is the rest "not our business?"

For better or worse the writer's only raw material is words. But whereas Eliot sees that material as elusive, escaping from his grasp even as he thinks to have it pinned, Edward Thomas adopts a more passive outlook, viewing himself as a humble instrument through which the words themselves find self-expression. Whilst Eliot regards words as intractable, Thomas seeks harmony with them; he wants them to choose him, to use him, to dance with him, to blend with him in ecstasy. Thomas clearly held language, especially the English language, as something inherently natural, even sacrosanct.

EDWARD THOMAS
Words

Out of us all
That make rhymes,
Will you choose
Sometimes—

As the winds use
A crack in a wall
Or a drain,
Their joy or their pain
To whistle through—
Choose me,
You English words?

I know you:
You are light as dreams,
Tough as oak,
Precious as gold,
As poppies and corn,
Or an old cloak:
Sweet as our birds
To the ear,
As the burnet rose
In the heat
Of Midsummer:
Strange as the races
Of dead and unborn:
Strange and sweet
Equally
And familiar,
To the eye,
As the dearest faces
That a man knows,
And as lost homes are:
But though older far
Than oldest yew,—
As our hills are, old,—
Worn new
Again and again:
Young as our streams
After rain:
And as dear
As the earth which you prove
That we love.

Make me content
With some sweetness
From Wales
Whose nightingales
Have no wings,—
From Wiltshire and Kent
And Herefordshire,
And the villages there,—
From the names, and the things
No less.
Let me sometimes dance
With you
Or climb
Or stand perchance
In ecstasy,
Fixed and free
In a rhyme,
As poets do.

Discussion topics

a. "Shabby equipment always deteriorating" or "Worn new again and again." Which poet do you support?

b. The Oxford English Dictionary defines "sentiment" as a "tendency to be swayed by feeling rather than reason, emotional weakness, mawkish tenderness." In that a poet is frequently swayed by emotion rather than reason, sentiment is inevitably present in much poetry. Such sentiment, however, may easily become "mawkish," (defined in turn by the OED as "feebly sentimental") and, as such, be justifiably criticised. Is the sentiment in *Words* under control?

c. Here is the third stanza of *Words* set out in normal prose paragraph shape:

> Make me content with some sweetness from Wales whose nightingales have no wings,—from Wiltshire and Kent and Herefordshire, and the villages there,—from the names, and the things no less. Let me sometimes dance with you or climb or stand perchance in ecstasy, fixed and free in a rhyme, as poets do.

What does Thomas achieve by adopting such unusual short lines for his stanzas?

Words are the raw material of any writer but that is only the beginning of the operation. Setting aside for the moment the

Brooke Church, Rutland.

"From this church they led their brides
From this church themselves were led
Shoulder-high"

E. Blunden p.37

poet's treatment of his theme we have first to consider his technique. No poet has a more delicate mastery of technique than Alexander Pope and it is instructive to watch him deploying his skills:

> But most by Numbers judge a Poet's song;
> And smooth or rough, with them, is right or wrong:
> In the bright Muse, tho' thousand charms conspire,
> Her voice is all these tuneful fools admire;
> Who haunt Parnassus but to please their ear,
> Not mend their minds: as some to church repair,
> Not for the doctrine, but the music there.
> These equal syllables alone require,
> Tho' oft the ear the open vowels tire;
> While expletives their feeble aid do join,
> And ten low words oft creep in one dull line:
> While they ring round the same unvary'd chimes,
> With sure returns of still expected rhymes:
> Where'er you find 'the cooling western breeze',
> In the next line, it 'whispers through the trees':
> If crystal streams 'with pleasing murmurs creep',
> The reader's threatened (not in vain) with 'sleep':
> Then, at the last and only couplet fraught
> With some unmeaning thing they call a thought,
> A heedless Alexandrine ends the song,
> That, like a wounded snake, drags its slow length along.
> . . . .
> True ease in writing comes from art, not chance,
> As those move easiest who here learned to dance.
> 'Tis not enough no harshness gives offence,
> The sound must seem an Echo to the sense;
> Soft is the strain when Zephyr gently blows,
> And the smooth stream in smoother numbers flows:
> But when loud surges lash the sounding shore,
> The hoarse, rough verse should like the torrent roar.
> When Ajax strives some rock's vast weight to throw,
> The line too labours, and the words move slow;
> Not so when swift Camilla scours the plain,
> Flies o'er th'unbending corn, and skims along the main.

Through subtle vowel and consonant interplay Pope achieves an astonishing rhythmic variety within the deliberate confines of the iambic pentameter, and this despite the punctuated end-stopping of each line and couplet. He avoids monotony, too, by a constant shifting of the caesura, some lines requiring a heavy caesura break after the second or third beats, some lines dispensing with the caesura altogether. It all looks so deceptively simple but it is indeed "art" not "chance" which contrives the effect. And it precisely meets Milton's definition of poetry, "Thoughts that voluntary move harmonious numbers."

> True Wit is Nature to advantage dressed;
> What oft was thought, but ne'er so well expressed.

Although Pope is defining wit rather than poetry (they virtually merged in the eighteenth century), it is instructive to compare Pope's view with Eliot's. Eliot appears to be striving for the unattainable in that ultimately poetry always eludes his grasp:

> And what there is to conquer
> By strength and submission, has already been discovered
> Once or twice, or several times, by men whom one cannot
>   hope
> To emulate—but there is no competition—
> There is only the fight to recover what has been lost
> And found and lost again and again. . . .

Pope, on the other hand, clearly holds that the poet is he who coins a new phrase for an old thought:

> Something, whose truth convinced at sight we find,
> That gives us back the image of the mind.

And what a master Pope was both in coining such phrases and in expressing the thought in balanced, condensed couplets.

To attempt to paraphrase some of his pithier couplets into prose is another instructive exercise in itself; the prose version is likely to be twice the length. Here are just three couplets for prose paraphrase.

> Words are like leaves, and where they most abound,
> Much fruit of sense beneath is rarely found.

or

'Tis with our judgments as our watches, none
Go just alike, yet each believes his own.

or

Envy will merit, as its shade, pursue,
But like a shadow, proves the substance true.

And has any writer ever defended rational compromise with
more perfect eloquence?

Avoid Extremes: and shun the fault of such
Who still are pleased too little or too much.
At every trifle scorn to take offence:
That always shows great pride, or little sense;
Those heads, as stomachs, are not sure the best
Which nauseate all, and nothing can digest.
Yet let not each gay Turn thy rapture move,
For fools admire, but men of sense approve:
As things seem large which we through mists descry,
Dulness is ever apt to magnify.

If, in the last resort, one criticises Pope for reflecting rather than
originating ideas, it is still fair to assert that he has given another
dimension to English literature, a dimension which has enriched
that literature in unique fashion. "There are many mansions in
poetry," the critic George Saintsbury once wrote, "and the great
poets live apart in them. What constitutes a great poet is supremacy in his own line of poetical expression." There is no doubt
of Pope's supremacy in his chosen genre of wit.

Since this book largely aspires to be an anthology of poetry
rather than of verse, it is time to attempt a definition of terms.
"Sir, what is poetry?" the indefatigable Boswell enquired of
Johnson, and even the redoubtable sage took refuge in his reply,
"Why, sir, it is much easier to say what it is not." As a start,
however, it may help to set alongside each other what is clearly
a piece of verse and then an example of poetry:

I put my hat upon my head and walked into the Strand
And there I met another man whose hat was in his hand

So much for the obvious verse, but this stanza from *The Rime of
the Ancient Mariner* is, as assuredly, poetry.

> A noise like of a hidden brook
> In the leafy month of June
> That to the quiet woods all night
> Singeth a quiet tune.

Back to verse:

> Here lies our flower, our little Nell:
> God thought he too would like a smell.

W. S. Landor's quatrain is poetry:

> I strove with none; for none was worth my strife;
> Nature I loved, and next to Nature, Art;
> I warmed both hands before the fire of life;
> It sinks, and I am ready to depart.

What essentially distinguishes poetry from verse is its quality of thought. "Poetry," Harold Nicolson once said, "elevates . . . it is the art form most essential to culture because it deepens feeling: the lanes which lead us to our deepest feelings have been plotted for us by the poets. They teach us how we should feel about great things. They express our ideals in their most memorable terms." And Hazlitt remarked that poetry was invented "to take the language of the imagination off the ground." In the same sense Ruskin would claim that poetry is the fine particle within us that "expands, rarefies, refines, and raises our whole being."

Which is not to say that verse cannot be great fun and possess a technical ingenuity of its own. No versifier has ever excelled W. S. Gilbert and countless examples of that ingenuity are displayed in his patter songs which, incidentally, also provide excellent scale practice for the reading aloud of verse . . . and, ultimately, poetry. They could be compared to a Czerny scale exercise for the pupil on the piano. Here, for example, is Gilbert's immortal Major-General from *The Pirates of Penzance*:

> I am the very pattern of a modern Major-Gineral,
> I've information vegetable, animal, and mineral;
> I know the Kings of England, and I quote the fights
>   historical,
> From Marathon to Waterloo, in order categorical;
> I'm very well acquainted, too, with matters mathematical,
> I understand equations, both the simple and quadratical;

About binomial theorem I'm teeming with a lot o' news,
With interesting facts about the square of the hypotenuse.
I'm very good at integral and differential calculus,
I know the scientific names of beings animalculus,
In short, in matters vegetable, animal, and mineral,
I am the very model of a modern Major-Gineral.

I know our mythic history . . . King Arthur's and Sir
    Caradoc's,
I answer hard acrostics, I've a pretty taste for paradox;
I quote in elegiacs all the crimes of Heliogabalus,
In conics I can floor peculiarities parabolous.
I can tell undoubted Raphaels from Gerard Dows and Zof-
    fanies,
I know the croaking chorus from the 'Frogs' of Aristo-
    phanes;
Then I can hum a fugue, of which I've heard the music's din
    afore,
And whistle all the airs from that infernal nonsense
    'Pinafore.'
Then I can write a washing-bill in Babylonic cuneiform,
And tell you every detail of Caractacus's uniform.
In short, in matters vegetable, animal, and mineral,
I am the very model of a modern Major-Gineral.

In fact, when I know what is meant by 'mamelon' and
    'ravelin,'
When I can tell at sight a Chassepot rifle from a javelin,
When such affairs as sorties and surprises I'm more wary at,
And when I know precisely what is meant by Commissariat,
When I have learnt what progress has been made in modern
    gunnery,
When I know more of tactics than a novice in a nunnery,
In short, when I've a smattering of elementary strategy,
You'll say a better Major-GenerAL has never SAT a gee—
For my military knowledge, though I'm plucky and ad-
    ventury,
Has only been brought down to the beginning of the
    century.
But still in learning vegetable, animal, and mineral,
I am the very model of a modern Major-Gineral.

Much of the humour in Gilbert's verse depends on the rippling polysyllabic rhythm which positively requires the verse to be read at a considerable pace in order to place two heavy stresses on the second and tenth syllables of each line. Technically, each line is of twelve syllables with eight iambic feet, e.g.

<blockquote>
1   2   3   4   5   6   7   8
I am / the ve / ry pat / tern of / a mod / ern Ma / jor-Gin / eral,
I've in / forma / tion ve / geta / ble, an / imal, / and min / eral,
</blockquote>

In fact it would be utterly absurd to read the verse in such fashion for an actual reading enforces a two-beat line with a ripple of short beats between:

<blockquote>
1 2 3   4 5 6 7   8 9 10 11   12 13 14 15 16
I am the very pattern of a modern Major-Gi ne ral
1   2 3 4 5   6 7 8 9 10 11 12   13   14 15 16
I've information vegetable, an i mal, and miner al.
</blockquote>

Part of the fun, too, lies in the way Gilbert forces the reader to give a word like "vegetable" four syllables in order to maintain the meticulous stresses of the ripple.

The verse of the American, Ogden Nash, also derives much of its humour from a play on rhymes. With Nash, however, it is the deliberate subordination of the metrical shape to the long-awaited rhyme which imparts the humour to his theme: the reader has to gabble the second line at top speed, whilst holding the rhyme of the first line in his mind's eye, in order ultimately to clinch the rhyme and the sense.

OGDEN NASH
England Expects

Let us pause to consider the English,
Who when they pause to consider themselves they get all
    reticently thrilled and tinglish.
Englishmen are distinguished by their traditions and cere-
    monials,
And also by their affection for their colonies and their con-
    descension to their colonials.

When foreigners ponder world affairs, why sometimes by
doubts they are smitten,

But Englishmen know instinctively that what the world
needs most is whatever is best for Great Britain.

English people disclaim sparkle and verve,

But speak without reservations of their Anglo-Saxon reserve.

After listening to little groups of English ladies and gentlemen at cocktail parties and in hotels and Pullmans,
of defining Anglo-Saxon reserve I despair,

But I think it consists of assuming that nobody else is there.

All good young Englishmen go to Oxford or Cambridge
and they all write and publish books before their grad-
uation,

And I often wondered how they did it until I realised that
they have to do it because their genteel accents are so
developed that they can no longer understand each
other's spoken words so the written word is their only
means of intercommunication.

England is the last home of the aristocracy, and the art of
protecting the aristocracy from the encroachments of
commerce has been raised to quite an art,

Because in America a rich butter-and-egg man is only a rich
butter-and-egg man or at most an honourary LL. D. of
some hungry university, but in England why before he
knows it he is Sir Benjamin Buttery, Bart.

Anyhow, I think the English people are sweet,

And we might as well get used to them because when they
slip and fall they always land on their own or somebody
else's feet.

"One thing is certain," James Reeves, poet and critic, once
wrote. "The primary purpose of poetry is magical . . . the desire
to communicate is the root from which all poetry springs. All
poetry has to do with communication but it is not merely *saying*
something in a special way . . . it is a special form of words which
has the power, magical power, to evoke certain responses in the
hearer or reader. Poetry is an intellectual manifestation of the
human spirit with the power to touch and disturb the reader's
thoughts." Magic is closely associated with fancy and the boundary

between them is often blurred. Edward Lear's *Nonsense Rhymes* fall within this no-man's land. Those who dismiss them as trivial verse fail to appreciate that his subtleties of rhythm, incantatory handling of refrains, and hallucinatory themes, embody flights of fancy which evoke in the perceptive reader a response which is essentially poetic. Incidentally, in Lear's hands, his spécialité de la maison, the Limerick, soars out of the sordid and smutty into delicious intellectual effervescence; it is so often the polysyllabic descriptive adjective in the final line which, above even the rhyming absurdity, especially delights the connoisseur ("that *accomplished* Young Lady of Welling . . . that *mendacious* Old Person of Gretna . . . that *dolorous* Man of Cape Horn"). No anthology of poetry is complete without a Lear limerick or two and one of his nonsense rhymes. Here, then, is an aperitif; one must hope that it will subsequently tempt the reader to venture on an à la carte choice for the main meal . . . and, of course, on Lear's unique illustrations which are essential complements to the poems.

> There was an Old Person of Spain,
> Who hated all trouble and pain;
>   So he sat on a chair,
>   With his feet in the air,
> That umbrageous Old Person of Spain.

> There was an Old Lady whose folly
> Induced her to sit in a holly;
>   Whereupon by a thorn
>   Her dress being torn,
> She quickly became melancholy.

> There was an Old Person of Tring
> Who embellished his nose with a ring;
>   He gazed at the moon
>   Every evening in June,
> That ecstatic Old Person of Tring.

For a Nonsense Rhyme my personal favourite remains the Pobble and his Aunt Jobiska.

EDWARD LEAR
The Pobble Who Has No Toes

The Pobble who has no toes
   Had once as many as we;
When they said, "Some day you may lose them all;"—
   He replied,—"Fish fiddle de-dee!"—
And his Aunt Jobiska made him drink,
Lavender water tinged with pink,
For she said, "The World in general knows
There's nothing so good for a Pobble's toes!"

The Pobble who has no toes,
   Swam across the Bristol Channel;
But before he set out he wrapped his nose
   In a piece of scarlet flannel.
For his Aunt Jobiska said, "No harm
Can come to his toes if his nose is warm;
And it's perfectly known that a Pobble's toes
Are safe,—provided he minds his nose—"

The Pobble swam fast and well,
   And when boats or ships came near him
He tinkledy-binkledy winkled a bell,
   So that all the world could hear him.
And all the Sailors and Admirals cried,
When they saw him nearing the further side,—
"He has gone to fish, for his Aunt Jobiska's
Runcible Cat with crimson whiskers."

But before he touched the shore,
   The shore of the Bristol Channel,
A sea-green Porpoise carried away
   His wrapper of scarlet flannel.
And when he came to observe his feet,
Formerly garnished with toes so neat,
His face at once became forlorn
On perceiving that all his toes were gone!

And nobody ever knew
  From that dark day to the present,
Whoso had taken the Pobble's toes,
  In a manner so far from pleasant.
Whether the shrimps or Crayfish gray,
Or crafty Mermaids stole them away—
Nobody knew; and nobody knows
How the Pobble was robbed of his twice five toes!

The Pobble who has no toes
  Was placed in a friendly Bark,
And they rowed him back, and carried him up,
  To his Aunt Jobiska's Park.
And she made him a feast at his earnest wish
Of eggs and buttercups fried with fish;—
And she said,—"It's a fact the whole world knows,
That Pobbles are happier without their toes."

Byron's poetry links the metrical skill of Gilbert to the pointed wit of Pope, and with a cynicism which is in no way dated; indeed, although *Don Juan* was written one hundred and fifty years ago, the sarcasm strikes as incisively and topically as the latest TV satirical show. Partly this is because Byron, in the aftermath of the French Revolution, was also living in an age of disillusionment and felt as keenly as ourselves the indignation of a cultured man in the face of what he felt to be a crumbling civilisation; and partly, I think, Byron's sophisticated contempt for the hypocrisy of reputation and power is frequently paralleled by twentieth-century writers. Here Byron meditates on the accidents of fame:

But words are things, and a small drop of ink,
Falling like dew, upon a thought, produces
That which makes thousands, perhaps millions, think;
'Tis strange, the shortest letter which man uses
Instead of speech, may form a lasting link
Of ages; to what straits old Time reduces
Frail man, when paper—even a rag like this,
Survives himself, his tomb, and all that's his.

And when his bones are dust, his grave a blank,
His station, generation, even his nation,
Become a thing, or nothing, save to rank
In chronological commemoration,
Some dull M.S. oblivion long has sank,
Or graven stone found in a barrack's station
In digging the foundation of a closet,
May turn his name up, as a rare deposit.

What is the end of fame? 'tis but to fill
A certain portion of uncertain paper:
Some liken it to climbing up a hill,
Whose summit, like all hills, is lost in vapour;
For this men write, speak, preach, and heroes kill,
And bards burn what they call their 'midnight taper,'
To have, when the original is dust,
A name, a wretched picture, and worse bust.

What are the hopes of man? Old Egypt's King
Cheops erected the first pyramid
And largest, thinking it was just the thing
To keep his memory whole, and mummy hid:
But somebody or other rummaging,
Burglariously broke his coffin's lid.
Let not a monument give you or me hopes,
Since not a pinch of dust remains of Cheops.

One of the best methods of analysing a poet's skill is to attempt to parody his style and Byron's stanza lends itself admirably to such an exercise. A slight alteration in the rhetorical question can start things off—"What is the end of School?" for example, or "What is the end of Sport?" The exercise will take the pupil into the poet's workshop and he will find it a challenging task to sustain a satirical viewpoint through the stanza, to contain it within the demanding rhyme scheme, and to point the moral with a satisfying clinching couplet. Byron's very success tends to make *Don Juan* difficult reading. Each stanza is such a satisfying unit in itself that the total overall momentum of the poem through several hundred lines and numerous stanzas is sometimes lost.

II

IMAGERY OF WORDS

Words, then, are the raw material of the poet and it is with words that he must necessarily wrestle in order to give metrical structure and form to his concepts. In this wrestling he displays his technique. But the poet is not only concerned with the sound, shape, and syllabic quantity of his words; above all else he is concerned with their meaning.

Now in discussing the meaning of a word we have to be aware of something highly important. This is the distinction between the objective and the subjective use of a word, between, on the one hand, its factual defining function and on the other the emotional connotations which it may suggest. Some words hardly lend themselves to anything other than objective use; the word "child," for example, is fairly neutral in its definitive terms; but if we call a child a "brat" or, alternatively, a "cherub," the words carry heavy emotional overtones. These overtones will vary subjectively with each individual but we can safely assume that for most people a "brat" carries unfavourable connotations whilst a "cherub" does the opposite. It is an illuminating exercise, indeed, to give a prose description of the image which each of these two words produces in the reader's mind.

Now although we all of us vary in our subjective and objective use of language—we should be dull speakers and writers if we did not—it is in poetry that we find language employed at its deepest subjective levels. And it is inevitable that this should be so. For the poet is endeavouring in his poetry to give significance to his experience and in so far as he succeeds it will be because he has captured in words some experience unique to himself which his art enables him to share with us, anyway in part. His experience will necessarily be subjective and is also likely to be imprecise; the poet will suggest rather than state, imply rather than direct, hint rather than express.

An appreciation of the difference between the objective and the subjective use of language is vital to a true understanding of poetry and its creation. It is therefore worth spending a little time on considering in detail some contrasting passages of objective and subjective writing. Here, then, are two straightforward pieces of objective writing:

> Weeds are a serious problem in any garden. They compete for plant nutrients and water in the soil and for space and light above ground. The weight of a barrow load of weeds is proof of how much they take from the soil. Weeds are vigorous and will take over completely if unchecked. A row of vegetable seedlings can easily be smothered by weeds which generally germinate and grow faster than cultivated plants. They also harbour pests and diseases during the winter. So one way and another, weeds must go.

The writer's directions to the vegetable grower as to how to beat weeds in the garden are positive, simple, and clear. The sentences may be somewhat monotonous in their subject + verb structure, but the verbs are direct and forceful ("compete" "unchecked" "smothered" "germinate" "harbour") whilst the nouns are also factual and precise ("problem" "nutrients" "space" "light" "weight" "pests" "diseases"). As one would expect from objective writing, few adjectives are employed for adjectives tend to be subjective words adding colour, tone and feeling to nouns and are unnecessary in this context where the nouns are conveying their unmistakeable message, "One way and another, weeds must go."

And here is the second objective passage:

> Mild weather in January will often trigger the first bursts of song from the common thrush, and because each phrase is repeated several times, it is probably the easiest to recognise of all garden bird songs. With four bright blue, blackspotted thrush's eggs against the unique mud lining, the song nest is an attractive sight. Unfortunately it is also easy to find and the species suffers nearly as badly as the blackbird from human predation.

Once again, this passage is characteristic of objective prose. The writer does, however, allow himself one subjective moment as the choice of one particular verb exemplifies. Which is that verb and what are its subjective implications? The reader who can answer that question satisfactorily is well on the way to understanding poetry and its creation.

And so to the subjective passage and pure poetry; here is Gerard Manley Hopkins treating the oldest of poetic themes—Spring—in unique and novel subjective fashion:

John o'Gaunt Viaduct

"What is this life, if full of care,
We have no time to stand and stare.
No time to stand beneath the boughs
And stare as long as sheep or cows".

W. H. Davies p.38

Nothing is so beautiful as spring—
   When weeds, in wheels, shoot long and lovely and lush;
   Thrush's eggs look little low heavens, and thrush
Through the echoing timber does so rinse and wring
The ear, it strikes like lightnings to hear him sing;
   The glassy pear-tree leaves and blooms, they brush
   The descending blue; that blue is all in a rush
With richness; the racing lambs too have fair their fling.

This is highly original subjective writing. Weeds, far from being things that "must go" symbolise the luscious growth of spring and are an inherent part of the "juice and joy" of that season. The thrush's song has the freshness of water and in this connection Hopkins makes dramatic use first of a tactile image ("rinse and wring") and then of a visual image ("strikes like lightnings") to describe the *sound* of the bird's song! He then coins a new verb (as a flower "blooms," so a leaf "leaves") to describe the leaves of the pear tree, mixing here a naturalist's objective accuracy with a poet's subjective imagination—the "glassy" leaves of the pear tree truthfully describe their reflective quality. The "descending blue" of the sky harks back to the thrush's eggs as being "little low heavens" and there is much repetition of the rich 'ush' sound from the opening lines. Indeed the sound effects add immeasurably to the poem's theme whether it be alliteration which Hopkins so freely employs (weeds / wheels, long / lovely / lush / look / little, blooms / brush / blue, rinse / wring) or assonance as in weeds / wheels, lovely / lush / thrush, timber / rinse / ring, strikes / lightnings, or consonance, e.g., glassy / leaves / blooms / blue.

The sounds, then, echo the sense but it is the sense which is truly poetic. Hopkins treats what many might consider the hackneyed theme of spring in a wholly new way; weeds are the embodiment of growth, the thrush's cerulean-blue eggs seem to come trailing clouds of glory from heaven, the thrush's song, limpid and lustrous in its liquidity, cleanses our inner ear even as it strikes to our heart; leaves and blossoms burgeon, heaven itself provides a blue enfolding background to all this rich growth, which embraces, too, the innocent high spirits of the animal kingdom ("the racing lambs too have fair their fling"). Yet even as one attempts to capture the poet's theme in prose it is obvious that the poetry is lost and refutes such analysis. For a prose paraphrase just cannot capture the evanescent quality of poetry; poetry, one must repeat, through the poet's subjective emotion, imagination, and feeling, hints, implies, suggests, and sets sounding in our minds reverberating chords of meditative thought. So the true poet sounds fresh chords and gives his topic a new significance which will enlarge the reader's total awareness of the world.

It is time, however, to consider the complete Hopkins sonnet:

> Nothing is so beautiful as spring—
>   When weeds, in wheels, shoot long and lovely and lush;
>   Thrush's eggs look little low heavens, and thrush
> Through the echoing timber does so rinse and wring
> The ear, it strikes like lightnings to hear him sing;
>   The glassy pear-tree leaves and blooms, they brush
>   The descending blue; that blue is all in a rush
> With richness; the racing lambs too have fair their fling.
>
> What is all this juice and all this joy?
>   A strain of the earth's sweet being in the beginning
> In Eden garden.—Have, get, before it cloy,
>   Before it cloud, Christ, Lord, and sour with sinning,
> Innocent mind and Mayday in girl and boy,
>   Most, O Maid's child, thy choice and worthy the winning.

Books have been written on the sonnet and on sonnet form. Sufficient here to observe that a sonnet is of fourteen lines length, with a rhythm of iambic pentameters, and that the Italian form of sonnet, from which the English sonnet first derived, normally consists of an octave plus sestet with a turn of thought (Italian 'volta') linking the two. The other common sonnet form is the English or Shakespearian, where the sonnet consists of three four-line sections (quatrains) and the volta then occurs in the shape of a clinching final rhyming couplet. In both sonnet forms strict rhyming is called for although the rhyme scheme can be very varied.

Hopkins, therefore, is here employing the Italian form of sonnet and the volta, as one might expect with a Jesuit priest, embodies a Christian turn of thought. First, Hopkins answers his own rhetorical question, "What is all this juice and all this joy?" by claiming that each Spring is a reincarnation in part of the Garden of Eden. As such, it is in one sense a personification of innocence, an innocence which should be immediately enjoyed for its own sake, the more so since such innocence can all too soon be contaminated by evil. Next, Hopkins likens this Garden of Eden innocence to the purity of young minds which in themselves most truly reflect Christ himself and should prove His most worthy disciples.

Hopkins' sonnet repays careful analysis for these fourteen lines are unmistakeable poetry. There could be no more hackneyed theme than that of Spring, nor, at a superficial level, more trite aspects of it than those selected by Hopkins—weeds, the thrush's nest and its song, fruit trees blossoming against a blue sky. Yet by his original treatment of these commonplaces of Spring Hopkins opens our eyes to novel aspects of this season of "juice and joy" and, by his philosophical sestet, provides an added religious significance. Anyone who has read and absorbed Hopkins' sonnet will find his awareness of Spring has been heightened; never again will his experience of that season be quite as it was before his reading of the poem. A new dimension has been added to his experience.

It is in his power to give significance to the everyday events of life that the poet displays his genius. The following winter poem of Thomas Hardy's, apart from serving as a fitting antithesis to Hopkins' sonnet, is another excellent illustration of this power.

Thomas Hardy
The Darkling Thrush

I leaned upon a coppice gate
  When Frost was spectre-gray,
And Winter's dregs made desolate
  The weakening eye of day.
The tangled bine-stems scored the sky
  Like strings from broken lyres,
And all mankind that haunted nigh
  Had sought their household fires.

The land's sharp features seemed to be
  The Century's corpse outleant;
His crypt the cloudy canopy,
  The wind his death-lament.
The ancient pulse of germ and birth
  Was shrunken hard and dry,
And every spirit upon earth
  Seemed fervourless as I.

At once a voice arose among
    The bleak twigs overhead
In a full-hearted evensong
    Of joy illimited;
An aged thrush, frail, gaunt and small,
    In blast-beruffled plume,
Had chosen thus to fling his soul
    Upon the growing gloom.

So little cause for carollings
    Of such ecstatic sound
Was written on terrestrial things
    Afar or nigh around,
That I could think there trembled through
    His happy good-night air
Some blessed Hope, whereof he knew
    And I was unaware.

The subjective use of words and imagery to create the desolate, dead winter scene is masterful; the emotive implications of "spectre-gray," "Winter's dregs," "weakening eye," "haunted," and the broken lyre metaphor set the scene most powerfully, a scene which the second stanza dramatically reinforces with the sustained simile of the "sharp features" of the "Century's corpse," its "crypt" and "death-lament" of clouds and wind, all leading to the shrunken, fervourless pulse of nature. In the third stanza the word "evensong" hints at a change of mood and carries interesting spiritual undertones which gain in strength as the gallant thrush "flings his soul" upon the "growing gloom": and the fourth stanza reinforces this trembling hope—an astonishing one, in view of Hardy's philosophy of an Indifferent Will pervading the universe—in moving, mysterious terms.

A sense of the mysterious regenerative power which informs all nature is again movingly illustrated by Edward Thomas in this simplest of poetic statements entitled *Thaw*:

Over the land freckled with snow half-thawed
The speculating rooks at their nests cawed
And saw from elm-tops, delicate as flower of grass,
What we below could not see, Winter pass.

As a true countryman no one savoured Spring with more genuine first-hand experience than Shakespeare: in Keats' fine phrase he felt it "along the pulse." Is there a more evocative phrase in all poetry than "Daffodils, that come before the swallow dares, and take the winds of March with beauty"? The song of the two pages in *As You Like It* is also pure lyrical delight:

WILLIAM SHAKESPEARE
Extract from *As You Like It*

It was a lover and his lass,
    With a hey, and a ho, and a hey nonino,
That o'er the green corn-field did pass,
    In the spring-time, the only pretty ring time,
When birds do sing, hey ding a ding, ding;
Sweet lovers love the spring.

Between the acres of the rye,
    With a hey, and a ho, and a hey nonino,
These pretty country folks would lie,
    In the spring-time, the only pretty ring time,
When birds do sing, hey ding a ding, ding;
Sweet lovers love the spring.

This carol they began that hour,
    With a hey, and a ho, and a hey nonino,
How that life was but a flower
    In the spring-time, the only pretty ring time,
When birds do sing, hey ding a ding, ding;
Sweet lovers love the spring.

And therefore take the present time
    With a hey, and a ho, and a hey nonino;
For love is crowned with the prime
    In the spring-time, the only pretty ring time,
When birds do sing, hey ding a ding, ding;
Sweet lovers love the spring.

III

THE HUMAN COMEDY

In a much-quoted definition Shelley called poets "the unacknowledged legislators of the world," and, commenting on this, James Kirkup, himself a poet, said, "By 'legislators' I do not understand Shelley to mean law-makers in the ordinary sense. I understand the poet as a spokesman of conscience, as one who remembers the heart of things, the patterns and rhythms of earth and nature, and all the indescribable mysteries of life, all those things that are beyond science and which our poets have come most near to understanding." I would agree with Kirkup that it is the poet, above anyone else in this irreligious twentieth century, who acts as "a spokesman of conscience" and approaches closest to "the heart of things." So this next group of poems reflects the poet's view of humanity and of the world in which, for better or for worse, humanity finds itself placed. Naturally, individual attitudes vary enormously and range from Browning's robust optimism to Macneice's cynical pessimism, from viewing man's life, with Thomas Hobbes, as "solitary, poor, nasty, brutish, and short" to Shelley's idyllic dream of eternity:

> The One remains, the many change and pass;
> Heaven's light forever shines, Earth's shadows fly;
> Life, like a dome of many-coloured glass,
> Stains the white radiance of Eternity.

Our first philosopher poet must be Shakespeare.

> All the world's a stage,
> And all the men and women merely players;
> They have their exits and their entrances;
> And one man in his time plays many parts,
> His acts being seven ages. As, first the infant
> Mewling and puking in the nurse's arms.
> And then the whining schoolboy, with his satchel
> And shining morning face, creeping like snail

Unwillingly to school. And then the lover,
Sighing like furnace, with a woeful ballad
Made to his mistress' eyebrow. Then the soldier
Full of strange oaths, and bearded like the pard,
Jealous in honour, sudden and quick in quarrel,
Seeking the bubble reputation
Even in the cannon's mouth. And then the justice,
In fair round belly with good capon lined,
With eyes severe and beard of formal cut,
Full of wise saws and modern instances;
And so he plays his part. The sixth age shifts
Into the lean and slipper'd pantaloon,
With spectacles on nose and pouch on side;
His youthful hose, well saved, a world too wide
For his shrunk shank; and his big manly voice,
Turning again toward childish treble, pipes
And whistles in his sound. Last scene of all,
That ends this strange eventful history,
Is second childishness and mere oblivion,
Sans teeth, sans eyes, sans taste, sans everything.

The following poem was said by Pope to have been written when he was "not twelve years old," although he revised it before he let it be printed. One wonders if Sir Henry Wotton's *The Happy Life*, with its well-known opening and closing stanzas served Pope as a model; Wotton's poem was written about a century earlier and begins:

How happy is he born and taught
  That serveth not another's will;
Whose armour is his honest thought,
  And simple truth his utmost skill!

The middle stanzas depict a man "whose conscience is his strong retreat" and the poem ends:

—This man is freed from servile bands
  Of hope to rise, or fear to fall:
Lord of himself, though not of lands;
  And having nothing, yet hath all.

ALEXANDER POPE
Ode on Solitude

Happy the man, whose wish and care
  A few paternal acres bound,
Content to breathe his native air,
    In his own ground.

Whose herds with milk, whose fields with bread,
  Whose flocks supply him with attire,
Whose trees in summer yield him shade,
    In winter fire.

Blest, who can unconcern'dly find
  Hours, days, and years slide soft away,
In health of body, peace of mind,
    Quiet by day,

Sound sleep by night; study and ease,
  Together mixt; sweet recreation;
And innocence, which most does please
    With meditation.

Thus let me live, unseen, unknown.
  Thus unlamented let me die,
Steal from the world, and not a stone
    Tell where I lie.

The dictionary defines an aphorism as a "precept expressed in few words; a maxim" and this poem reveals Pope's aphoristic skill from a tender age. Technically he achieves some of his compressive skill by ellipsis, that is by omitting unnecessary repetition of a verb, e.g. "supply" and "yield" in the second stanza; or one preposition is made to govern a number of nouns, e.g. in the third stanza where the preposition "in" governs a whole list of nouns running on into the next stanza, "health," "peace," "quiet," "sleep," "study," "ease," "recreation," and "innocence"; or, by inverting the usual subject-verb-object order Pope makes his point more succinctly, e.g., "whose wish and care a few paternal acres bound." Still on technicalities, the sound perfectly echoes the sense and this is especially true of the two final stanzas. The soft *s* and *c* sounds in the fourth stanza, the labials in the fifth, and the long *ee* vowel sound in both these stanzas are all equally appropriate.

Discussion topics

a. How do the open vowel rhymes contribute to the mood of the poem (e.g. care/air, attire/fire, die/lie)?

b. Pope makes much use of enjambement, that is, running over of lines either from one line to the next or even from one stanza to the next. Does this have an effect on the poem?

c. Analyse the poem's metre. Why do you think Pope indents the lines as he does? What, in particular, is the effect of the short final line in each stanza?

d. The poem is without any imagery of metaphor or simile; adjectives are used sparingly. In what way, then, does Pope's vocabulary achieve his desired effects?

Johnson praised Gray's *Elegy Written in a Country Churchyard* as abounding "with images which find a mirror in every mind, and with sentiments to which every bosom returns an echo." By symbolising general themes through particular images (elms and yews=country tradition and peaceful death; swallow's nest and housewife's hearth=fruitful life; cockrow and horn, sickle and ploughing=native energy), Gray gives our common homely experiences an added dimension and induces the reader to stand aside from his day-to-day routine for a few moments and weigh the ultimate truths of existence.

THOMAS GRAY
Extracts from *An Elegy Written in a Country Churchyard*

The Curfew tolls the knell of parting day,
  The lowing herd wind slowly o'er the lea,
The plowman homeward plods his weary way,
  And leaves the world to darkness and to me.

Now fades the glimmering landscape on the sight,
  And all the air a solemn stillness holds,
Save where the beetle wheels his droning flight,
  And drowsy tinklings lull the distant folds;

Save that from yonder ivy-mantled tow'r
  The moping owl does to the moon complain
Of such as, wand'ring near her secret bow'r,
  Molest her ancient solitary reign.

Owston Church: Sunset

"A serious house on serious earth it is,
In whose blent air all our compulsions meet,
Are recognised, and robed as destines."

Beneath those rugged elms, that yew-tree's shade,
  Where heaves the turf in many a mould'ring heap,
Each in his narrow cell for ever laid,
  The rude Forefathers of the hamlet sleep.

The breezy call of incense-breathing Morn,
  The swallow twitt'ring from the straw-built shed,
The cock's shrill clarion, or the echoing horn,
  No more shall rouse them from their lowly bed.

For them no more the blazing hearth shall burn,
  Or busy housewife ply her evening care:
No children run to lisp their sire's return,
  Or climb his knees the envied kiss to share.

Oft did the harvest to their sickle yield,
  Their furrow oft the stubborn glebe has broke:
How jocund did they drive their team afield!
  How bow'd the woods beneath their sturdy stroke!

Let not Ambition mock their useful toil,
  Their homely joys, and destiny obscure;
Nor Grandeur hear with a disdainful smile
  The short and simple annals of the poor.

The boast of heraldry, the pomp of pow'r,
  And all that beauty, all that wealth e'er gave,
Awaits alike th' inevitable hour:
  The paths of glory lead but to the grave.

Nor you, ye Proud, impute to These the fault,
  If Memory o'er their Tomb no Trophies raise,
Where through the long-drawn aisle and fretted vault
  The pealing anthem swells the note of praise.

Can storied urn or animated bust
  Back to its mansion call the fleeting breath?
Can Honour's voice provoke the silent dust,
  Or Flatt'ry soothe the dull cold ear of death?

Perhaps in this neglected spot is laid
  Some heart once pregnant with celestial fire;
Hands, that the rod of empire might have sway'd,
  Or waked to ecstasy the living lyre.

But Knowledge to their eyes her ample page
   Rich with the spoils of time did ne'er unroll;
Chill Penury repress'd their noble rage,
   And froze the genial current of the soul.

Full many a gem of purest ray serene
   The dark unfathom'd caves of ocean bear:
Full many a flower is born to blush unseen,
   And waste its sweetness on the desert air.

Some village Hampden that with dauntless breast
   The little tyrant of his fields withstood,
Some mute inglorious Milton here may rest,
   Some Cromwell guiltless of his country's blood.
. . . .
Far from the madding crowd's ignoble strife
   Their sober wishes never learn'd to stray;
Along the cool sequester'd vale of life
   They kept the noiseless tenor of their way.

Yet ev'n these bones from insult to protect
   Some frail memorial still erected nigh,
With uncouth rhymes and shapeless sculpture deck'd,
   Implores the passing tribute of a sigh.
. . . .
For who, to dumb Forgetfulness a prey,
   This pleasing anxious being e'er resign'd,
Left the warm precincts of the cheerful day,
   Nor cast one longing ling'ring look behind?

On some fond breast the parting soul relies,
   Some pious drops the closing eye requires;
E'en from the tomb the voice of Nature cries,
   E'en in our Ashes live their wonted Fires.

To attempt an appreciation of a poem in isolation is often difficult; it frequently helps if two poems can be contrasted and my next poem, Edmund Blunden's *Forefathers*, directly invites comparison with Gray's *Elegy*. What is the point of departure of each poem? To what extent does each poet involve himself in the situation? Do they select similar imagery and employ it in much the same way? Do the moods of the poems differ? Which stanza form appears most appropriate to the theme? Is it fair to say that both poets deviate from their initial theme? Can you establish a preference as between the poems? If so, why?

EDMUND BLUNDEN
Forefathers

Here they went with smock and crook,
    Toil'd in the sun, loll'd in the shade,
Here they mudded out the brook
    And here their hatchet clear'd the glade:
Harvest-supper woke their wit,
Huntsman's moon their wooings lit.

From this church they led their brides,
    From this church themselves were led
Shoulder-high; on these waysides
    Sat to take their beer and bread.
Names are gone—what men they were
These their cottages declare.

Names are vanish'd, save the few
    In the old brown Bible scrawl'd;
These were men of pith and thew
    Whom the city never call'd;
Scarce could read or hold a quill,
Built the barn, the forge, the mill.

On the green they watch'd their sons
    Playing till too dark to see,
As their fathers watch'd them once,
    As my father once watch'd me;
While the bat and beetle flew
On the warm air webb'd with dew.

Unrecorded, unrenown'd,
    Men from whom my ways begin,
Here I know you by your ground
    But I know you not within—
There is silence, there survives
Not a moment of your lives.

Like the bee that now is blown
　Honey-heavy on my hand,
From his toppling tansy-throne
　In the green tempestuous land—
I'm in clover now, nor know
Who made honey long ago.

W. H. Davies, author of that unique book, *The Autobiography of a Super-Tramp*, which contains a notable description of his foot being severed from his leg whilst he attempted to jump a ride on a train, produced a small number of poems which are deceptively simple yet evoke deep feeling. Although Davies could well have been excused had "chill penury" frozen "the genial current of his soul," he retained a cheerful naiveté and a spontaneous sense of wonder for the world about him which were happily manifested in his poetry.

W. H. DAVIES
Leisure

What is this life if, full of care,
We have no time to stand and stare?—

No time to stand beneath the boughs
And stare as long as sheep or cows:

No time to see, when woods we pass,
Where squirrels hide their nuts in grass:

No time to see, in broad daylight,
Streams full of stars, like skies at night:

No time to turn at Beauty's glance,
And watch her feet, how they can dance:

No time to wait till her mouth can
Enrich that smile her eyes began?

A poor life this if, full of care,
We have no time to stand and stare.

WILLIAM SHAKESPEARE
Macbeth's Final Soliloquy

To-morrow, and to-morrow, and to-morrow,
Creeps in this petty pace from day to day,
To the last syllable of recorded time;
And all our yesterdays have lighted fools
The way to dusty death. Out, out, brief candle!
Life's but a walking shadow; a poor player,
That struts and frets his hour upon the stage,
And then is heard no more; it is a tale
Told by an idiot, full of sound and fury,
Signifying nothing.

In his great work on *Civilisation*, Sir Kenneth Clark observes of Shakespeare: "In his freedom of mind, in his power of self-identification, in his complete absence of any dogma, Shakespeare sums up and illuminates the Renaissance. . . . He must be the first and may be the last supremely great poet to have been without a religious belief, even without the humanist's belief in man . . . there have been great pessimists since his time but who else has felt so strongly the absolute meaningless of life?" Clark then quotes the Macbeth speech and concludes " . . . yet I feel that the human mind has gained a new greatness by outstaring this experience."

LOUIS MACNEICE
Sunday Morning

Down the road someone is practising scales,
The notes like little fishes vanish with a wink of tails,
Man's heart expands to tinker with his car
For this is Sunday morning, Fate's great bazaar;
Regard these means as ends, concentrate on this Now,
And you may grow to music or drive beyond Hindhead
    anyhow,
Take corners on two wheels until you go so fast
That you can clutch a fringe or two of the windy past,
That you can abstract this day and make it to the week of
    time
A small eternity, a sonnet self-contained in rhyme.

But listen, up the road, something gulps, the church spire
Opens its eight bells out, skulls' mouths which will not tire
To tell how there is no music or movement which secures
Escape from the weekday time. Which deadens and endures.

This is a powerful sonnet which demands to be read aloud so
that full force can be given to the measured pulse of time in the
final quatrain. It is essential, too, to grasp the poet's entire meaning. Why, for example, is Sunday morning described as "Fate's
great bazaar?" Why a capital "Now?" What does Macneice mean
by "grow to music" and why "Hindhead?" Can you offer a guess
about "a fringe or two of the windy past?" Finally, what is the
force of "skulls' mouths?"

MATTHEW ARNOLD

Extracts from *The Scholar Gypsy*

The poet is comparing the scholar gypsy's untrammelled acceptance
of life with our own uncertainties, hesitations and "light half-beliefs"
in "our casual creeds."

For early didst thou leave the world, with powers
   Fresh, undiverted to the world without,
     Firm to their mark, not spent on other things;
   Free from the sick fatigue, the languid doubt,
     Which much to have tried, in much been baffled, brings.
       O Life unlike to ours!
Who fluctuate idly without term or scope,
     Of whom each strives, nor knows for what he strives,
     And each half lives a hundred different lives;
   Who wait like thee, but not, like thee, in hope.

Thou waitest for the spark from Heaven: and we,
   Vague half-believers of our casual creeds,
     Who never deeply felt, nor clearly will'd,
   Whose insight never has borne fruit in deeds,
     Whose weak resolves never have been fulfill'd;
       For whom each year we see
Breeds new beginnings, disappointments new;
     Who hesitate and falter life away,
     And lose to-morrow the ground won to-day—
Ah, do not we, Wanderer, await it too?

O born in days when wits were fresh and clear,
  And life ran gaily as the sparkling Thames;
    Before this strange disease of modern life,
  With its sick hurry, its divided aims,
    Its heads o'ertaxed, its palsied hearts, was rife—
      Fly hence, our contact fear!
  Still fly, plunge deeper in the bowering wood!
    Averse, as Dido did with gesture stern
    From her false friend's approach in Hades turn,
  Wave us away, and keep thy solitude.

Still nursing the unconquerable hope,
  Still clutching the inviolable shade,
    With a free onward impulse brushing through,
  By night, the silver'd branches of the glade—
    Far on the forest-skirts, where none pursue,
      On some mild pastoral slope
  Emerge, and resting on the moonlit pales,
    Freshen thy flowers, as in former years,
    With dew, or listen with enchanted ears,
  From the dark dingles, to the nightingales.

PHILIP LARKIN
Church Going

Once I am sure there's nothing going on
I step inside, letting the door thud shut.
Another church: matting, seats, and stone,
And little books; sprawlings of flowers, cut
For Sunday, brownish now; some brass and stuff
Up at the holy end; the small neat organ;
And a tense, musty, unignorable silence.
Brewed God knows how long. Hatless, I take off
My cycle-clips in awkward reverence,

Move forward, run my hand around the font.
From where I stand, the roof looks almost new—
Cleaned, or restored? Someone would know: I don't.
Mounting the lectern, I peruse a few

Hectoring large-scale verses, and pronounce
'Here endeth' much more loudly than I'd meant.
The echoes snigger briefly. Back at the door
I sign the book, donate an Irish sixpence,
Reflect the place was not worth stopping for.

Yet stop I did: in fact I often do,
And always end much at a loss like this,
Wondering what to look for; wondering, too,
When churches fall completely out of use
What we shall turn them into, if we shall keep
A few cathedrals chronically on show,
Their parchment, plate and pyx in locked cases,
And let the rest rent-free to rain and sheep.
Shall we avoid them as unlucky places?

Or, after dark, will dubious women come
To make their children touch a particular stone;
Pick simples for a cancer; or on some
Advised night see walking a dead one?
Power of some sort or other will go on
In games, in riddles, seemingly at random;
But superstition, like belief, must die,
And what remains when disbelief has gone?
Grass, weedy pavement, brambles, buttress, sky.

A shape less recognisable each week,
A purpose more obscure. I wonder who
Will be the last, the very last, to seek
This place for what it was; one of the crew
That tap and jot and know what rood-lofts were?
Some ruin-bibber, randy for antique,
Or Christmas-addict, counting on a whiff
Of gown-and-bands and organ-pipes and myrrh?
Or will he be my representative,

Bored, uninformed, knowing the ghostly silt
Dispersed, yet tending to this cross of ground
Through suburb scrub because it held unspilt
So long and equably what since is found
Only in separation—marriage, and birth,
And death, and thoughts of these—for whom was built

This special shell? For though I've no idea
What this accoutred frosty barn is worth,
It pleases me to stand in silence here;

A serious house on serious earth it is,
In whose blent air all our compulsions meet,
Are recognised, and robed as destinies.
And that much never can be obsolete,
Since someone will forever be surprising
A hunger in himself to be more serious,
And gravitating with it to this ground,
Which, he once heard, was proper to grow wise in,
If only that so many dead lie round.

In this poem Larkin successfully portrays the pathetic attempts of twentieth-century man to glimpse some religious truths in the Christian church where he may occasionally worship and where he will almost certainly expect to be baptised, married, and buried. Although the tone of the poem is self-deprecatory and the language may on a first reading seem deliberately conversational, even casual, closer study reveals a serious spiritual involvement beneath the surface. An element of mystery pervades the poem from the "tense, musty, unignorable silence, brewed God knows how long" through "the echoes snigger," "the dubious women," "the purpose more obscure," "the ghostly silt dispersed" and "this accoutred frosty barn." The last stanza compresses in a powerful statement our instinctive religious yearnings for a church and its ceremonial:

A serious house on serious earth it is,
In whose blent air all our compulsions meet,
Are recognised, and robed as destinies.

Finally, the inspired use of the word "gravitating" leads us pointedly to the sombre conclusion.

LOUIS MACNEICE
Bagpipe Music

It's no go the merry-go-round, it's no go the rickshaw,
All we want is a limousine and a ticket for the peepshow.

Their knickers are made of crêpe-de-chine, their shoes are
    made of python,
Their halls are lined with tiger rugs and their walls with
    heads of bison.

John MacDonald found a corpse, put it under the sofa,
Waited till it came to life and hit it with a poker,
Sold its eyes for souvenirs, sold its blood for whiskey,
Kept its bones for dumb-bells to use when he was fifty.

It's no go the Yogi-Man, it's no go Blavatsky,
All we want is a bank balance and a bit of skirt in a taxi.

Annie MacDougall went to milk, caught her foot in the
    heather,
Woke to hear a dance record playing of Old Vienna.
It's no go your maidenheads, it's no go your culture,
All we want is a Dunlop tyre and the devil mend the
    puncture.

The Laird o' Phelps spent Hogmanay declaring he was sober,
Counted his feet to prove the fact and found he had one
    foot over.
Mrs Carmichael had her fifth, looked at the job with
    repulsion,
Said to the midwife, 'Take it away; I'm through with over
    production.'

It's no go the gossip column, it's no go the Ceilidh,
All we want is a mother's help and a sugar-stick for the
    baby.

Willie Murray cut his thumb, couldn't count the damage,
Took the hide of an Ayrshire cow and used it for a bandage.
His brother caught three hundred cran when the seas were
    lavish,
Threw the bleeders back in the sea and went upon the parish.

It's no go the Herring Board, it's no go the Bible,
All we want is a packet of fags when our hands are idle.

It's no go the picture palace, it's no go the stadium,
It's no go the country cot with a pot of pink geraniums,
It's no go the Government grants, it's no go the elections,
Sit on your arse for fifty years and hang your hat on a
pension.

It's no go my honey love, it's no go my poppet;
Work your hands from day to day, the winds will blow the
profit.
The glass is falling hour by hour, the glass will fall for ever,
But if you break the bloody glass you won't hold up the
weather.

G. M. HOPKINS
God's Grandeur

The world is charged with the grandeur of God.
  It will flame out, like shining from shook foil;
  It gathers to a greatness, like the ooze of oil
Crushed. Why do men then now not reck his rod?
Generations have trod, have trod, have trod;
  And all is smeared with trade; bleared, smeared with toil;
  And wears man's smudge and shares man's smell: the soil
Is bare now, nor can foot feel, being shod.

And for all this, nature is never spent;
  There lives the dearest freshness deep down things;
And though the last lights off the black West went
  Oh, morning, at the brown brink eastward, springs—
Because the Holy Ghost over the bent
  World broods with warm breast and with ah! bright wings.

LOUIS UNTERMEYER
Portrait of a Machine

What nudity as beautiful as this
Obedient monster purring at its toil;
Those naked iron muscles dripping oil,
And the sure-fingered rods that never miss?
This long and shining flank of metal is
Magic that greasy labour cannot spoil;

While this vast engine that could rend the soil
Conceals its fury with a gentle hiss.

It does not vent its loathing, it does not turn
Upon its makers with destroying hate.
It bears a deeper malice; lives to earn
Its master's bread and laughs to see this great
Lord of the earth, who rules but cannot learn,
Become the slave of what his slaves create.

Discussion topics

a. What differing attitudes to technology do Untermeyer and Hopkins display? With which view are you most in sympathy? Why?

b. Both poets have chosen the sonnet form as the structure within which to shape their poetic thoughts. Explain upon what 'turn of thought' each poem pivots.

c. Comment on Untermeyer's use of personification. How does it help the impression he is trying to convey?

d. Analyse, by detailed quotation, the use Hopkins makes of assonance, consonance, and alliteration and try to show how their combined use add to the poem's impact.

The Coming of the King

(Scholars believe this impressive poem was written in the seventeenth century, but it cannot be certainly assigned to a specific poet.)

Yet if His Majesty, our sovereign Lord,
Should of his own accord
Friendly himself invite,
And say, "I'll be your guest to-morrow night,"
How should we stir ourselves, call and command
All hands to work! "Let no man idle stand!

"Set me fine Spanish tables in the hall;
See they be fitted all;
Let there be room to eat
And order taken that there want no meat.
See every sconce and candlestick made bright,
That without tapers they may give a light.

"Look to the presence. Are the carpets spread?
The dais o'er the head?
The cushions in the chairs,
And all the candles lighted on the stairs?
Perfume the chambers, and in any case
Let each man give attendance in his place!"

Thus if a King were coming, would we do;
And 'twere good reason, too.
For 'tis a duteous thing
To show all honour to an earthly king,
And after all our travail and our cost
So he be pleased, to think no labour lost.

But at the coming of the King of Heaven,
All's set at six and seven;
We wallow in our sin.
Christ cannot find a chamber in the inn.
We entertain Him always like a stranger,
And, as at first, still lodge Him in the manger.

STEPHEN SPENDER
The Landscape Near an Aerodrome

More beautiful and soft than any moth
With burring furred antennae feeling its huge path
Through dusk, the air liner with shut-off engines
Glides over suburbs and the sleeves set trailing tall
To point the wind. Gently, broadly, she falls,
Scarcely disturbing charted currents of air.

Lulled by descent, the travellers across sea
And across feminine land indulging its easy limbs
In miles of softness, now let their eyes trained by watching
Penetrate through dusk the outskirts of this town
Here where industry shows a fraying edge.
Here they may see what is being done.

Beyond the winking masthead light
And the landing ground, they observe the outposts

Of work: chimneys like lank black fingers
Or figures, frightening and mad: and squat buildings
With their strange air behind trees, like women's faces
Shattered by grief. Here where few houses
Moan with faint stars behind their blinds,
They remark the unhomely sense of complaint, like a dog
Shut out, and shivering at the foreign moon.

In the last sweep of life, they pass over fields
Behind the aerodrome, where boys play all day
Hacking dead grass: whose cries, like wild birds,
Settle upon the nearest roofs
But soon are hid under the loud city.

Then, as they land, they hear the tolling bell
Reaching across the landscape of hysteria,
To where, louder than all the charcoaled batteries
And imaged towers against that dying sky,
Religion stands, the Church blocking the sun.

Discussion topics

a. Examine and comment upon the moth image in the first stanza. Is it appropriate to the scene which the poet is describing?

b. Why does Spender call the land "feminine?" Does he sustain this image in any way?

c. What is the force of the "fraying edge of industry?"

d. Can you explain how "squat buildings" can be held to look "like women's faces shattered by grief," or how houses "moan with faint stars?"

e. How can a dog "shut out and shivering" be compared with "an unhomely smell of complaint?"

f. Why is the moon called "foreign?"

g. In the fourth stanza how does Spender convey a sense of distaste for the fields behind the aerodrome?

h. From a phrase in the final stanza suggest an alternative title for the poem. Why do you think Spender was so non-committal in his actual title?

i. Summarise the theme of the poem in about forty of your own words.

1584–1984
Oakham 12 Uppingham 14
The Quatercentenary Match
between the sister foundations

"If you can meet with Triumph and Disaster
And treat those two imposters just the same"

R. Kipling p.50

Rudyard Kipling had a remarkable feel for the spirit of his age and an equally remarkable flair for expressing that "zeitgeist" in the jargon of his day. Because any age tends to react strongly in taste against its immediate predecessor, Kipling's reputation presently stands at a low ebb—he died in 1936 during the Abdication crisis. Further, Kipling championed causes by which we are now embarrassed—imperialism, the officer caste, patriotism, the concept of an élite, and even his *Barrack-Room Ballads*, which depict so vividly the nineteenth-century long-service British mercenary army, are spoilt by an underlying air of patronage for Tommy Atkins. In a perceptive essay on Kipling, George Orwell summed him up as a "good bad poet" and added, "A good bad poem is a graceful monument to the obvious. It records in memorable form—for verse is a mnemonic device, amongst other things— some emotion which nearly every human being can share." It is this aspect of Kipling which Orwell had in mind when he reminded his reader of the number of commonly quoted phrases which Kipling has added to our language. Here are a selection:

"East is East, and West is West, and never the twain shall meet."
"And a woman is only a woman, but a good cigar is a smoke."
"What should they know of England who only England know?"
"You're a better man than I am Gunga Din."
"For the Colonel's lady and Judy O'Grady are sisters under the skin."
"Pull out, pull out, on the Long Trail—the trail that is always new."
"On the road to Mandalay, where the flying fishes play."
"Ship me somewheres East of Suez, where the best is like the worst."

Of all the examples of Kipling's good-bad poetry, as defined by Orwell, *If* is surely supreme. But however ingenious Orwell's argument—and the essay should be read in full—I must register my humble disagreement with it. No less a poet than Samuel Taylor Coleridge defined poetry as "the best words in the best order" and the Oxford English Dictionary calls poetry "the elevated expression of elevated thought or feeling in metrical form." Poetry has also been described as "sustained rhythmic speech patterns which evoke a powerful physical or emotional response." I would concur with all these attempts to define poetry and I believe that it is just because *If* so abundantly satisfies these criteria that it has achieved such popularity and, as an ironic result, become hackneyed through thoughtless repetition. If the reader will approach the poem without preconceived notions and examine the truths it expresses afresh, then the rhythmic pulse of the poem, like the rhythmic pulse of the *Authorised Version of the Bible* (which Kipling's work so often echoes) will merge with the thought to evoke a "physical or emotional response" from the reader.

RUDYARD KIPLING
If (from *Rewards and Fairies*)

If you can keep your head when all about you
    Are losing theirs and blaming it on you,
If you can trust yourself when all men doubt you,
    But make allowance for their doubting too;
If you can wait and not be tired by waiting,
    Or being lied about, don't deal in lies,
Or, being hated, don't give way to hating,
    And yet don't look too good, nor talk too wise:

If you can dream—and not make dreams your master;
    If you can think—and not make thoughts your aim;
If you can meet with Triumph and Disaster
    And treat those two imposters just the same;
If you can bear to hear the truth you've spoken
    Twisted by knaves to make a trap for fools,
Or watch the things you gave your life to, broken,
    And stoop and build 'em up with worn-out tools.

If you can make one heap of all your winnings
    And risk it on one turn of pitch and toss,
And lose, and start again at your beginnings
    And never breathe a word about your loss;
If you can force your heart and nerve and sinew
    To serve your turn long after they are gone,
And so hold on when there is nothing in you
    Except the Will which says to them: ' Hold on! '

If you can talk with crowds and keep your virtue,
    Or walk with kings—nor lose the common touch,

If neither foes nor loving friends can hurt you,
  If all men count with you, but none too much;
If you can fill the unforgiving minute
  With sixty seconds' worth of distance run,
Yours is the Earth and everything that's in it,
  And—which is more—you'll be a Man, my son!

PHILIP LARKIN
Poetry of Departures

Sometimes you hear, fifth-hand,
As epitaph:
'He chucked up everything
And just cleared off,'
And always the voice will sound
Certain you approve
This audacious, purifying,
Elemental move.

And they are right, I think.
We all hate home
And having to be there:
I detest my room,
Its specially-chosen junk,
The good books, the good bed,
And my life, in perfect order:
So to hear it said

'He walked out on the whole crowd'
Leaves me flushed and stirred,
Like 'Then she undid her dress'
Or 'Take that you bastard;'
Surely I can, if he did?
And that helps me stay
Sober and industrious.
But I'd go today,

Yes, swagger the nut-strewn roads,
Crouch in the fo'c'sle
Stubbly with goodness, if

It weren't so artificial,
Such a deliberate step backwards
To create an object:
Books; china; a life
Reprehensibly perfect.

Larkin's poems often seem to involve a strenuous intellectual wrestling with an idea; a train of logical thought proceeds in ordered steps but frequently ends in a complex fall. So it is with this poem—the final stanza demands careful analysis for Larkin's precise meaning.

LOUIS MACNEICE
Explorations

The whale butting through scarps of moving marble,
The tapeworm probing the intestinal darkness,
The swallows drawn collectively to their magnet,
   These are our prototypes and yet,
Though we may envy them still, they are merely patterns
   To wonder at—and forget.

For the ocean-carver, cumbrous but unencumbered,
Who tired of land looked for his freedom and frolic in water,
Though he succeeded, has failed; it is only instinct
   That plots his graph and he,
Though appearing to us a free and happy monster, is merely
   An appanage of the sea.

And the colourless blind worm, triumphantly self-degraded,
Who serves as an image to man of the worst adjustment—
Oxymoron of parasitical glory—
   Cannot even be cursed,
Lacking the only pride of his way, of life, not knowing
   That he has chosen the worst.

So even that legion of birds who appear so gladly
Purposeful, with air in their bones, enfranchised
Citizens of the sky and never at odds with

The season or out of line,
Can be no model to us; their imputed purpose
    Is a foregone design—

And ours is not.   For we are unique, a conscious
Hoping and therefore despairing creature, the final
Anomaly of the world, we can learn no method
    From whales or birds or worms;
Our end is our own to be won by our own endeavour
    And held on our own terms.

G. M. HOPKINS
Thou Art Indeed Just, Lord

Thou art indeed just, Lord, if I contend
With thee; but, Sir, so what I plead is just.
Why do sinners' ways prosper? and why must
Disappointment all I endeavour end?
    Wert thou my enemy, O thou my friend,
How wouldst thou worse, I wonder, than thou dost
Defeat, thwart me? Oh, the sots and thralls of lust
Do in spare hours more thrive than I that spend,
Sir, life upon thy cause. See, banks and brakes
Now, leavèd how thick! Lacèd they are again
With fretty chervil, look, and fresh wind shakes
Them; birds build—but not I build; no, but strain,
Time's eunuch, and not breed one work that wakes.
Mine, O thou lord of life, send my roots rain.

This is one of the great group of Hopkins "despair" sonnets where
he gives vent to his bitterness not so much for a loss of inspiration
as for the total neglect of his creative genius. I have James Reeves
to thank for pointing out a remarkable parallel in Coleridge's
Work Without Hope:

All Nature seems at work. Slugs leave their lair—
The bees are stirring—birds are on the wing—
And Winter slumbering in the open air,
Wears on his smiling face a dream of Spring!
And I the while, the sole unbusy thing,
Nor honey make nor pair, nor build, nor sing.

And Wordsworth's *Ode to Immortality*, of course, is concerned
with the same theme:

> There was a time when meadow, grove, and stream,
> The earth, and every common sight,
> To me did seem
> Apparelled in celestial light,
> The glory and the freshness of a dream.
> It is not now as it hath been of yore—
> Turn wheresoe'er I may,
> By night or day,
> The things which I have seen I now can see no more.
>
> The rainbow comes and goes,
> And lovely is the rose,
> The moon doth with delight
> Look round her when the heavens are bare,
> Waters on a starry night
> Are beautiful and fair;
> The sunshine is a glorious birth;
> But yet I know, where'er I go,
> That there hath passed away a glory from the earth.
> . . . .
> Our birth is but a sleep and a forgetting:
> The soul that rises with us, our life's star,
> Hath had elsewhere its setting,
> And cometh from afar;
> Not in entire forgetfulness,
> And not in utter nakedness,
> But trailing clouds of glory do we come
> From God, who is our home.
> Heaven lies about us in our infancy;
> Shades of the prison-house begin to close
> Upon the growing boy,
> But he beholds the light, and whence it flows.
> He sees it in his joy;
> The youth, who daily farther from the east
> Must travel, still is Nature's priest,
> And by the vision splendid
> Is on his way attended;

At length the man perceives it die away,
And fade into the light of common day.

JOHN KEATS
Stanzas

In a drear-nighted December,
   Too happy, happy tree,
Thy branches ne'er remember
   Their green felicity:
The north cannot undo them,
With a sleety whistle through them;
Nor frozen thawings glue them
   From budding at the prime.

In a drear-nighted December,
   Too happy, happy brook,
Thy bubblings ne'er remember
   Apollo's summer look;
But with a sweet forgetting,
They stay their crystal fretting,
Never, never petting
   About the frozen time.

Ah! would 'twere so with many
   A gentle girl and boy!
But were there ever any
   Writhed not at passéd joy?
To know the change and feel it,
When there is none to heal it,
Nor numbéd sense to steel it,
   Was never said in rhyme.

IV

PLACE

V. SACKVILLE-WEST
Extracts from *The Land*

The country habit has me by the heart,
For he's bewitched forever who has seen,
Not with his eyes but with his vision, Spring
Flow down the woods and stipple leaves with sun,
As each man knows the life that fits him best,
The shape it makes in his soul, the tune, the tone,
And after ranging on a tentative flight
Stoops like the merlin to the constant lure.
The country habit has me by the heart.
I never hear the sheep-bells in the fold,
Nor see the ungainly heron rise and flap
Over the marsh, nor hear the asprous corn
Clash, as the reapers set the sheaves in shocks
(That like a tented army dream away
The night beneath the moon in silvered fields),
Nor watch the stubborn team of horse and man
Graven upon the skyline, nor regain
The sign-posts on the road towards my home
Bearing familiar names—without a strong
Leaping of recognition; only here
Lies peace after uneasy truancy;
Here meet and marry many harmonies,
—All harmonies being ultimately one,—
Small mirroring majestic; for as earth
Rolls on her journey, so her little fields
Ripen or sleep, and the necessities
Of seasons match the planetary law.
So truly stride between the earth and heaven
Sowers of grain: so truly in the spring
Earth's orbit swings both blood and sap to rhythm,
And infinite and humble are at one;

So the brown hedger, through the evening lanes
Homeward returning, sees above the ricks,
Sickle in hand, the sickle in the sky.

Shepherds and stars are quiet with the hills.
There is a bond between the men who go
From youth about the business of the earth,
And the earth they serve, their cradle and their grave;
Stars with the seasons alter; only he
Who wakeful follows the pricked revolving sky,
Turns concordant with the earth while others sleep;
To him the dawn is punctual; to him
The quarters of the year no empty name.
A brutish life, but in the midst of dark
Cut to a gash of beauty, as when the hawk
Bears upwards in its talons the striking snake,
High, and yet higher, till those two hang close,
Sculptural on the blue, together twined,
Exalted, deathly, silent, and alone.

S. T. COLERIDGE
Extract from *Frost at Midnight*

The frost performs its secret ministry,
Unhelped by any wind. The owlet's cry
Came loud—and hark, again! loud as before.
The inmates of my cottage, all at rest,
Have left me to that solitude, which suits
Abstruser musings: save that at my side
My cradled infant slumbers peacefully.
'Tis calm indeed! so calm, that it disturbs
And vexes meditation with its strange
And extreme silentness. Sea, hill, and wood,
This populous village! Sea, and hill, and wood,
With all the numberless goings on of life,
Incredible as dreams! the thin blue flame
Lies on my low burnt fire, and quivers not;
Only that film, which fluttered on the grate,
Still flutters there, the sole unquiet thing.

Walter de la Mare's poetry possesses a unique ethereal haunting quality. His imagination was especially stirred by twilight or moonlight which allow perception only "through a glass darkly"; fully to appreciate the delicate sensitivity of his poetry the reader must approach it with tremulous antennae.

WALTER DE LA MARE
All That's Past

Very old are the woods;
  And the buds that break
Out of the brier's boughs,
  When March winds wake,
So old with their beauty are—
  Oh, no man knows
Through what wild centuries
  Roves back the rose.

Very old are the brooks;
  And the rills that rise
Where snow sleeps cold beneath
  The azure skies
Sing such a history
  Of come and gone,
Their every drop is as wise
  As Solomon.

Very old are we men;
  Our dreams are tales
Told in dim Eden
  By Eve's nightingales;
We wake and whisper awhile,
  But, the day gone by,
Silence and sleep like fields
  Of amaranth lie.

Discussion topics

a. There are several phrases in this poem which could serve as examples of "pure poetry." Which do you consider the supreme example? Why?

b. Why do you suppose Walter de la Mare adopted an eight instead of a four line stanza?

c. To what extent does the sound echo the sense? Examine, particularly, Walter de la Mare's control of assonance.

d. The poem ends on an open vowel sound. Does this make for any particular effect?

EDWARD THOMAS
Adlestrop

Yes, I remember Adlestrop—
The name, because one afternoon
Of heat the express-train drew up there
Unwontedly. It was late June.

The steam hissed. Someone cleared his throat.
No one left and no one came
On the bare platform. What I saw
Was Adlestrop—only the name

And willows, willow-herb, and grass,
And meadowsweet, and haycocks dry,
No whit less still and lonely fair
Than the high cloudlets in the sky.

And for that minute a blackbird sang
Close by, and round him, mistier,
Farther and farther, all the birds
Of Oxfordshire and Gloucestershire.

ROBERT BROWNING
Meeting at Night

I

The grey sea and the long black land;
And the yellow half-moon large and low;
And the startled little waves that leap
In fiery ringlets from their sleep,
As I gain the cove with pushing prow
And quench its speed i' the slushy sand.

II

Then a mile of warm sea-scented beach;
Three fields to cross till a farm appears;
A tap at the pane, the quick sharp scratch
And blue spurt of a lighted match,
And a voice less loud, thro' its joys and fears,
Than the two hearts beating each to each!

There is a fresh spontaneity about this poem which has survived
a hundred years. The air of romantic excitement and mystery are
quietly conveyed both by the sharp visual imagery, the colour
tones, and the contrasts of a rhythm which shifts from the hurrying
anapaests ($\smile\smile-$) of "and the yellow . . . and the startled . . . as I
gain . . . then a mile . . . and a voice" to the heavy spondees($--$)
of "grey sea—black land—half-moon—blue spurt—two hearts."
The diction is simple yet every word makes its impact—"quench,"
"tap," "scratch," and "spurt" being particularly effective. Finally, by
apt use of alliteration and consonance the sounds of the poem echo
most effectively the sense.

It is now nearly fifty years since A. E. Housman delivered his
famous lecture at Cambridge on The Name and Nature of Poetry.
That lecture remains a valuable insight into the genesis of poetry
in that Housman, a practising poet, described the actual processes,
both mental and physical, which he underwent in composing a
poem. First, however, he attempted his own definition of poetry.
Having dismissed John Gilpin as obvious verse, he quoted this
stanza from Samuel Daniel, a contemporary of Shakespeare's:

Come, worthy Greek, Ulysses, come,
    Possess these shores with me;
The winds and seas are troublesome,
    And here we may be free.
Here may we sit and view their toil
    That travail in the deep,
And joy the day in mirth the while,
    And spend the night in sleep.

"Diction and movement alike," commented Housman, "it is
perfect. It is made out of the most ordinary words; yet it is pure

from the least alloy of prose . . . but Poetry is capable of more than this pure language and liquid versification and the simple, colourless pleasure which they afford. . . . Poetry involves the presence of something which moves and touches (us) in a special and recognisable way," and he went on to quote these lines to a cuckoo by an eighteenth-century poet, John Logan:

> Sweet bird, thy bower is ever green,
> Thy sky is ever clear;
> Thou hast no sorrow in thy song,
> Nor winter in thy ear.

"A new element has stolen in," Housman continued, "a tinge of emotion. And I think that to transfuse emotion—not to transmit thought but to set up in the reader's sense a vibration corresponding to what was felt by the writer—is the peculiar function of poetry." Finally, he asserted that under these criteria even a brief phrase is immediately recognisable as poetry:

> . . . Duncan is in his grave;
> After life's fitful fever he sleeps well.

For myself, a quatrain by an anonymous poet and dating, possibly, from the sixteenth century, illustrates poetry and its power to transfuse emotion even more effectively than Daniel's lines:

> Western wind, when wilt thou blow,
> The small rain down can rain?
> Christ, if my love were in my arms
> And I in my bed again.

There is a cry of anguish in these lines that seems to strike freshly down the waste of three hundred years.

Housman's definition, however, is of great interest for the stress he places on the emotional, even physical, content of poetry. For he claimed that poetry was to him more physical than intellectual and he described how if a line of poetry came into his thoughts whilst he was shaving his skin actually bristled sufficiently to stop the razor acting. Just as Wordsworth described poetry as "the spontaneous overflow of powerful feelings" so Housman admitted that for him the production of poetry was, on occasion anyway, "more an involuntary and passive process than an active one." He then proceeded to enlarge on this process in a fascinating

account: "Having drunk a pint of beer at luncheon—beer is a
sedative to the brain, and my afternoons are the least intellectual
portion of my life—I would go for a walk of two or three hours.
As I went along, thinking of nothing in particular, only looking
at things around me and following the progress of the seasons,
there would flow into my mind, with sudden and unaccountable
emotion, sometimes a line or two of verse, sometimes a whole
stanza at once, accompanied, not preceded, by a vague notion of
the poem which they were destined to form part of. There would
usually be a lull of an hour or so, then perhaps the spring would
bubble up again. I say bubble up because, so far as I could make
out, the source of the suggestions . . . to the brain was . . . the pit
of the stomach. When I got home I wrote them down, leaving
gaps, and hoping that further inspiration might be forthcoming
another day. Sometimes it was, if I took my walks in a receptive
and expectant frame of mind; but sometimes the poem had to be
taken in hand and completed by the brain, which was apt to be a
matter of trouble and anxiety, involving trial and disappointment,
and sometimes ending in failure."

Housman then recounted the process of germination so far as
the following poem (LXIII in *A Shropshire Lad*) was concerned:
" Two of the stanzas, I do not say which, came into my head just
as they are printed, while I was crossing the corner of Hampstead
Heath between the Spaniard's Inn and the footpath to Temple
Fortune. A third stanza came with a little coaxing after tea.
One more was needed, but it did not come: I had to turn to and
compose it myself, and that was a laborious business. I wrote it
thirteen times, and it was more than a twelvemonth before I got
it right." Here is Housman's poem. To attempt to establish the
two immediate stanzas, the "coaxing" stanza, and the "laborious"
one, makes an interesting exercise.

> I hoed and trenched and weeded,
> And took the flowers to fair;
> I brought them home unheeded;
> The hue was not the wear.
>
> So up and down I sow them
> For lads like me to find,
> When I shall lie below them,
> A dead man out of mind.

Some seed the birds devour,
    And some the season mars,
But here and there will flower
    The solitary stars,

And fields will yearly bear them
    As light-leaved spring comes on,
And luckless lads will wear them
    When I am dead and gone.

A. E. HOUSMAN
On Wenlock Edge
(Poem XXI, *A Shropshire Lad*)

On Wenlock Edge the wood's in trouble;
    His forest fleece the Wrekin heaves;
The gale, it plies the saplings double,
    And thick on Severn snow the leaves.

'Twould blow like this through holt and hanger
    When Uricon the city stood:
'Tis the old wind in the old anger,
    But then it threshed another wood.

Then, 'twas before my time, the Roman
    At yonder heaving hill would stare:
The blood that warms an English yeoman,
    The thoughts that hurt him, they were there.

There, like the wind through woods in riot,
    Through him the gale of life blew high;
The tree of man was never quiet:
    Then 'twas the Roman, now 'tis I.

The gale, it plies the saplings double,
    It blows so hard, 'twill soon be gone:
To-day the Roman and his trouble
    Are ashes under Uricon.

SIR JOHN BETJEMAN
Upper Lambourne

Up the ash-tree climbs the ivy,
　Up the ivy climbs the sun,
With a twenty-thousand pattering
　Has a valley breeze begun,
Feathery ash, neglected elder,
　Shift the shade and make it run—

Shift the shade toward the nettles,
　And the nettles set it free
To streak the stained Carrara headstone
　Where, in nineteen-twenty-three,
He who trained a hundred winners
　Paid the Final Entrance Fee.

Leathery limbs of Upper Lambourne,
　Leathery skin from sun and wind,
Leathery breeches, spreading stables,
　Shining saddles left behind—
To the down the string of horses
　Moving out of sight and mind.

Feathery ash in leathery Lambourne
　Waves above the sarson stone
And Edwardian plantations
　So coniferously moan
As to make the swelling downland,
　Far-surrounding, seem their own.

PHILIP LARKIN
At Grass

The eye can hardly pick them out
From the cold shade they shelter in,
Till wind distresses tail and mane;
Then one crops grass, and moves about
—The other seeming to look on—
And stands anonymous again.

Yet fifteen years ago, perhaps
Two dozen distances sufficed
To fable them: faint afternoons
Of Cups and Stakes and Handicaps,
Whereby their names were artificed
To inlay faded, classic Junes—

Silks at the start: against the sky
Numbers and parasols: outside,
Squadrons of empty cars, and heat,
And littered grass: then the long cry
Hanging unhushed till it subside
To stop-press columns on the street.

Do memories plague their ears like flies?
They shake their heads. Dusk brims the shadows.
Summer by summer all stole away,
The starting-gates, the crowds and cries—
All but the unmolesting meadows.
Almanacked, their names live; they

Have slipped their names, and stand at ease,
Or gallop for what must be joy,
And not a fieldglass sees them home,
Or curious stop-watch prophesies:
Only the groom, and the groom's boy,
With bridles in the evening come.

SIR JOHN BETJEMAN
Middlesex

Gaily into Ruislip Gardens
    Runs the red electric train,
With a thousand Ta's and Pardon's
    Daintily alights Elaine;
Hurries down the concrete station
With a frown of concentration,
Out into the outskirt's edges
Where a few surviving hedges
Keep alive our lost Elysium—rural Middlesex again.

Well cut Windsmoor flapping lightly,
    Jacqmar scarf of mauve and green
Hiding hair which, Friday nightly,
    Delicately drowns in Drene;
Fair Elaine the bobby-soxer,
Fresh complexioned with Innoxa,
Gains the garden—father's hobby—
Hangs her Windsmoor in the lobby,
Settles down to sandwich supper and the television screen.

Gentle Brent, I used to know you
    Wandering Wembley-wards at will,
Now what change your waters show you
    In the meadow-lands you fill!
Recollect the elm-trees misty
And the footpaths climbing twisty
Under cedar-shaded palings
Low laburnum-leaned-on railings,
Out of Northolt on and upward to the heights of Harrow hill.

Parish of enormous hayfields
    Perivale stood all alone,
And from Greenford scent of mayfields
    Most enticingly was blown
Over market gardens tidy,
Taverns for the bona-fide,
Cockney anglers, cockney shooters,
Murray Poshes, Lupin Pooters
Long in Kensal Green and Highgate silent under soot and stone.

Betjeman's banter conceals a consummate art. First, there is
his unique skill in the brush-strokes of topical detail which enables
him to render an immediate, vivid, and relevant picture of his
subject whether it be Elaine, the river Brent, or Perivale. By his
accurate pinpointing of Elaine's attire and accessories—the Windsmoor coat, the Jacqmar scarf, the Drene shampoo and Innoxa
cream—he establishes immediately her social level and way of life.
Then, he holds the shape of his thought taut and tantalising by
periodic rather than loose sentence structure, the conclusion of
each stanza (and some individual phrases) being adroitly withheld
to the final line. Then there is his art of compression:

Hiding hair which, Friday nightly,
   Delicately drowns in Drene;

or

Recollect the elm-trees misty
And the footpaths climbing twisty
Under cedar-shaded palings
Low laburnum-leaned-on railings,

or

Taverns for the bona-fide.

So much is said in the minimum of space and it is said so mel-
lifluously! It is this mellifluous quality of Betjeman's poetry, the
delicate rhythm rippling through the musical, almost magical,
control of vowel and consonant sounds, which imparts an overall
tone and tune to the poem and which creates the dominating mood
of nostaliga for the lost Elysium of Middlesex, whether rural or
suburban.

ROBERT BROWNING
"De Gustibus—"

Your ghost will walk, you lover of trees,
   (If our loves remain)
   In an English lane,
By a cornfield-side a-flutter with poppies.
Hark, those two in the hazel coppice—
A boy and a girl, if the good fates please,
   Making love, say,—
   The happier they!
Draw yourself up from the light of the moon,
And let them pass, as they will too soon,
   With the bean-flowers' boon,
   And the blackbird's tune,
   And May, and June!

What I love best in all the world,
Is a castle, precipice-encurled,
In a gash of the wind-grieved Appenine.
Or look for me, old fellow of mine,
(If I get my head from out the mouth

O' the grave, and loose my spirit's bands,
And come again to the land of lands)—
In a sea-side house to the farther South,
Where the baked cicalas die of drouth,
And one sharp tree—'tis a cypress—stands,
By the many hundred years red-rusted,
Rough iron-spiked, ripe fruit-o'ercrusted,
My sentinel to guard the sands
To the water's edge. For, what expands
Before the house, but the great opaque
Blue breadth of sea without a break?
While, in the house, for ever crumbles
Some fragment of the frescoed walls,
From blisters where a scorpion sprawls.
A girl bare-footed brings, and tumbles
Down on the pavement, green-flesh melons,
And says there's news to-day—the King
Was shot at, touched in the liver-wing,
Goes with his Bourbon arm in a sling:
—She hopes they have not caught the felons.
    Italy, my Italy!
Queen Mary's saying serves for me—
    (When fortune's malice
    Lost her Calais)
Open my heart and you will see
Graved inside of it, " Italy."
Such lovers old are I and she;
So it always was, so shall ever be!

WILLIAM COWPER
The Poplar-Field

The poplars are felled, farewell to the shade
And the whispering sound of the cool colonnade,
The winds play no longer, and sing in the leaves,
Nor Ouse on his bosom their image receives.

Twelve years have elapsed since I first took a view
Of my favourite field and the bank where they grew,
And now in the grass behold they are laid,
And the tree is my seat that once lent me a shade.

The blackbird has fled to another retreat
Where the hazels afford him a screen from the heat,
And the scene where his melody charmed me before,
Resounds with his sweet-flowing ditty no more.

My fugitive years are all hasting away,
And I must ere long lie as lowly as they,
With a turf on my breast, and a stone at my head,
Ere another such grove shall arise in its stead.

'Tis a sight to engage me, if any thing can,
To muse on the perishing pleasures of man;
Though his life be a dream, his enjoyments, I see,
Have a being less durable even than he.

In *The Stricken Deer*, his great biography of William Cowper, Lord David Cecil gives a fascinating account of how the quiet Buckinghamshire countryside around Olney did so much to heal Cowper's tormented spirit after one of his worst descents into a melancholic madness that had held him in a distorted religious despair for two years. What Cowper's spirit needed was calm and certainty and this was what the natural scene provided. In Lord David Cecil's own words: "Natural beauty belonged to that part of life into which the dismal problems of the soul did not enter . . . it had no need of a remoter charm ungathered from the eye and asked for its appreciation only the immediate instinctive pleasure that it stimulated. Indeed his enjoyment gained an exquisite, intolerable poignancy from his conviction that it had no significance in that world of spiritual values which, in his view, was the only reality, that all this tangible, palpable ravishing beauty he saw around him was really but the shadow of a shade, which within a few brief years would be lost to him for ever. . . . Cowper's love of Nature was . . . an affection rather than a passion."

Before considering to what extent *The Poplar-Field* confirms Lord David Cecil's analysis, it may be helpful to set alongside Cowper's poem the following poem by Gerard Manley Hopkins.

G. M. Hopkins
Binsey Poplars
felled 1879

My aspens dear, whose airy cages quelled,
Quelled or quenched in leaves the leaping sun,
All felled, felled, are all felled;
   Of a fresh and following folded rank
      Not spared, not one
       That dandled a sandalled
     Shadow that swam or sank
On meadow and river and wind-wandering weed-winding
   bank.

O if we but knew what we do
    When we delve or hew—
  Hack and rack the growing green!
     Since country is so tender
   To touch, her being so slender,
  That, like this sleek and seeing ball
  But a prick will make no eye at all,
  Where we, even where we mean
      To mend her we end her,
    When we hew or delve:
After-comers cannot guess the beauty been.
  Ten or twelve, only ten or twelve
    Strokes of havoc unselve
     The sweet especial scene,
    Rural scene, a rural scene,
    Sweet especial rural scene.

The underlying theme of this poem, that the wanton destroyer of the poplars has "unselved" a rural scene, can only be fully understood in relation to Hopkins' notion of "inscape." In brief, Hopkins was convinced that all things, whether animate or inanimate, possessed an essential form and that this form was significant of God's presence in the world. This "inscape" expressed, as it were, the inner soul of natural objects or scenes; the flight of a bird, for example, has its unique "inscape," as has the form of a leaf or tree, the force of the wind, or the moisture of the dew. Man, in Hopkins' view, tends to play the vandal in that he destroys the "inscape" of a scene by, for example, polluting the air with factory smoke or encircling mediaeval Oxford with squalid buildings or, as in this poem, felling a grove of poplars. So, whereas nature was to Cowper "an affection rather than a passion," it is fair to state that with Hopkins the reverse was the case.

Hopkins was intensely interested in language and was acutely conscious in his choice of vocabulary of the Classical, Hebrew, Saxon, or Welsh derivations of the words he might be employing. So, in *Binsey Poplars*, the effect of the word "quelled" and its rhyming with the repeated "felled" to echo the sound of the tree-felling, are enhanced when we realise that in German the word "quellen" means to cut. And reading the poem, as Hopkins always required his reader to do, with the whole understanding geared to the ear, one can almost detect a *v* sound in the "quelled," derived from the German pronunciation of "quellen," a sound that reappears in the word " delve " in the second stanza.

Discussion topics

a. The sound and rhythmic effects in *Binsey Poplars* give an added dimension to the theme. Show, by a detailed analysis, how such effects enhance
    (i) the river scene;
    (ii) the delicacy of the pastoral "inscape."

b. Explain the impact of the "eye" image.

c. Rhythm also plays a dominant role in Cowper's *Poplar-Field*. Surprisingly, for a meditative poem, the basic rhythmic pulse is in triple time. Comment in detail on the total rhythmic effects of the poem.

d. "Hopkins' love of Nature was passionate, Cowper's merely affectionate." Justify your agreement or disagreement with this statement by a detailed comparison of the poems.

V
WINE

THOMAS HARDY
Great Things

Sweet cyder is a great thing,
  A great thing to me,
Spinning down to Weymouth town
  By Ridgway thirstily,
And maid and mistress summoning
  Who tend the hostelry:
O cyder is a great thing,
  A great thing to me!

The dance it is a great thing,
  A great thing to me,
With candles lit and partners fit
  For night-long revelry;
And going home when day-dawning
  Peeps pale upon the lea:
O dancing is a great thing,
  A great thing to me!

Love is, yea, a great thing,
  A great thing to me,
When, having drawn across the lawn
  In darkness silently,
A figure flits like one a-wing
  Out from the nearest tree:
O love is, yes, a great thing,
  A great thing to me!

Will these be always great things,
  Great things to me?. . . .
Let it befall that One will call,
  'Soul, I have need of thee:'

What then? Joy-jaunts, impassioned flings,
   Love, and its ecstasy,
Will always have been great things,
   Great things to me!

HILAIRE BELLOC
Tarantella

Do you remember an Inn,
Miranda?
Do you remember an Inn?
And the tedding and the spreading
Of the straw for a bedding,
And the fleas that tease in the High Pyrenees,
And the wine that tasted of the tar,
And the cheers and the jeers of the young muleteers
(Under the vine of the dark verandah)?
Do you remember an Inn, Miranda,
Do you remember an Inn?
And the cheers and the jeers of the young muleteers
Who hadn't got a penny,
And who weren't paying any,
And the hammer at the doors and the Din?
And the Hip! Hop! Hap!
Of the clap
Of the hands to the twirl and the swirl
Of the girl gone chancing,
Glancing,
Dancing,
Backing and advancing,
Snapping of the clapper to the spin
Out and in—
And the Ting, Tong, Tang of the Guitar!
Do you remember an Inn,
Miranda?
Do you remember an Inn?
Never more;
Miranda,
Never more.
Only the high peaks hoar:

And Aragon a torrent at the door.
No sound
In the walls of the Halls where falls
The tread
Of the feet of the dead to the ground.
No sound:
But the boom
Of the far Waterfall like Doom.

Belloc's great friend and Catholic-in-arms was G. K. Chesterton, a personality who was larger than life. I remember his visiting Stowe to lecture to us, a mountain of a man, shuffling and wheezing, but with a high-pitched treble voice which added to the general ludicrous physical picture. Totally other-worldly and forgetful, his wife once received a telegram from him, stranded on a lecture tour, "Am in Market Harborough: where should I be?" His talk was brilliant, however, and shot through with paradoxes. "If a thing is worth doing, it's worth doing badly . . . one is company, two is none . . . art is limitation: the most beautiful part of any picture is the frame." He was, from all accounts, a gloriously rombustious character who shared, with Dr Johnson, a deep inner religious seriousness touched, one suspects, with a vein of melancholy. In both these poems Chesterton appears to joke when he is in earnest and the rombustious tone must not be allowed to obscure his serious purpose. Again, like Johnson, Chesterton mixed religious awe and a sense of sin with laughter, a gusto for life, and the love of friends.

G. K. CHESTERTON
The Rolling English Road

Before the Roman came to Rye or out to Severn strode,
The rolling English drunkard made the rolling English road.
A reeling road, a rolling road, that rambles round the shire,
And after him the parson ran, the sexton and the squire;
A merry road, a mazy road, and such as we did tread
The night we went to Birmingham by way of Beachy Head.

I knew no harm of Bonaparte and plenty of the Squire,
And for to fight the Frenchman I did not much desire;
But I did bash their baggonets because they came array'd
To straighten out the crooked road an English drunkard
    made,
Where you and I went down the lane with ale-mugs in our
    hands,
The night we went to Glastonbury by way of Goodwin
    Sands.

His sins they were forgiven him; or why do flowers run
Behind him; and the hedges all strengthening in the sun?
The wild thing went from left to right and knew not which
    was which,
But the wild rose was above him when they found him in
    the ditch.
God pardon us, nor harden us; we did not see so clear
The night we went to Bannockburn by way of Brighton
    Pier.

My friends, we will not go again or ape an ancient range,
Or stretch the folly of our youth to be the shame of age,
But walk with clearer eyes and ears this path that wandereth,
And see undrugg'd in evening light the decent inn of death;
For there is good news yet to hear and fine things to be seen,
Before we go to Paradise by way of Kensal Green.

G. K. CHESTERTON
The Good Rich Man

Mr Mandragon, the Millionaire, he wouldn't have wine or
    wife,
He couldn't endure complexity: he lived the Simple Life.
He ordered his lunch by megaphone in manly, simple tones,
And used all his motors for canvassing voters, and twenty
    telephones;
Besides a dandy little machine,
Cunning and neat as ever was seen,
With a hundred pulleys and cranks between,
Made of metal and kept quite clean,

Typical Leicestershire landscape on
the gated road leading home to Owston.

"The country habit has me by the heart"

V. Sackville-West p.59

To hoist him out of his healthful bed on every day of his
    life,
And wash him and dress him and shave him and brush him
    —to live the Simple Life.

Mr Mandragon was most refined and quietly, neatly dressed,
Say all the American newspapers that know refinement best;
Quiet and neat the hat and hair and the coat quiet and neat,
A trouser worn upon either leg, while boots adorn the feet;
And not, as any one would expect,
A Tiger's skin all striped and specked,
And a Peacock Hat with the tail erect,
A scarlet tunic with sunflowers decked,
Which might have had a more marked effect,
And pleased the pride of a weaker man that yearned for
    wine or wife;
But Fame and the Flagon for Mr Mandragon
    —obscured the Simple Life.

Mr Mandragon, the Millionaire, I am happy to say, is dead;
He enjoyed a quiet funeral in a crematorium shed.
And he lies there fluffy and soft and grey and certainly
    quite refined;
When he might have rotted to flowers and fruit with Adam
    and all mankind,
Or been eaten by wolves athirst for blood,
Or burnt on a good tall pyre of wood,
In a towering flame, as a heathen should,
Or even sat with us here at food,
Merrily taking twopenny ale and pork with a pocket-knife;
But this was luxury not for one that went for the Simple
    Life.

HILAIRE BELLOC
Concluding lines of *An Heroic Poem in Praise of Wine*

When from the waste of such long labour done
I too must leave the grape-ennobling sun
And like the vineyard worker take my way
Down the long shadows of declining day,

Bend on the sombre plain my clouded sight
And leave the mountain to the advancing night,
Come to the term of all that was mine own
With nothingness before me, and alone;
Then to what hope of answer shall I turn?
Comrade-Commander whom I dared not earn,
What said You then to trembling friends and few?

"A moment, and I drink it with you new:
But in my Father's kingdom." So, my Friend,
Let not Your cup desert me in the end.
But when the hour of mine adventure's near
Just and benignant, let my youth appear
Bearing a Chalice, open, golden, wide,
With benediction graven on its side.
So touch my dying lip: so bridge that deep:
So pledge my waking from the gift of sleep,
And, sacramental, raise me the Divine:
Strong brother in God and last companion, Wine.

VI

WOMEN

Thomas Hardy's pilgrimage to Cornwall in order to carry out an architectural survey of St Juliot's church, near Boscastle, besides being notable for the rich poetic documentation with which he has adorned it, is now established as a famous piece of English literary folk-lore. It was on a raw Monday morning, March 7, 1870, that Hardy, then aged twenty-nine, rose at half-past three by candle-light at his thatched birthplace cottage at Upper Bockhampton on the edge of Puddletown Heath, Dorset, in order to set out on an hour's walk to catch an early morning connection at Dorchester for the first stage of his train journey, which involved changes at Yeovil and Exeter, to Launceston. From Launceston a horse-drawn four-wheeler took him the final fifteen miles to St Juliot rectory. The Cornish roads were primitive, the lanes narrow and the hills steep, so that this part of his journey took several hours and darkness had descended when, at the end of an especially narrow and embanked lane, he at last reached the rectory. Hardy was at once admitted by the maid and introduced to the rector's sister-in-law, Miss Emma Lavinia Gifford. Carl J. Weber takes up the story in his *Hardy's Love Poems*. "Miss Gifford noticed Hardy's soft voice, his slightly different accent, his beard, which made him look older than he really was, and his rather shabby overcoat: she noticed, too, that there was a blue paper sticking out of his pocket. She thought it might be a design for the church-tower but Hardy informed her that it was the manuscript of a poem."

After three days work on St Juliot's church Hardy undertook the equally daunting journey home but although his relationship with Miss Gifford had not yet reached a formal engagement stage there was no doubt in Hardy's mind that he had met his wife-to-be. Those four days at St Juliot, which were followed by several subsequent visits, were a turning point in his life and led to that subsequent—and tragic—marriage four years later. But in the halcyon afterglow of his first meeting with Emma, Hardy wrote

the first of the many poems which were to derive their inspiration
from Emma and her Cornish environment:

When I set out for Lyonnesse
  A hundred miles away,
  The rime was on the spray,
And starlight lit my lonesomeness
When I set out for Lyonnesse
  A hundred miles away.

What would perchance at Lyonnesse
  While I should sojourn there
  No prophet durst declare,
Nor did the wisest wizard guess
What would perchance at Lyonnesse
  While I should sojourn there.

When I came back from Lyonnesse
  With magic in my eyes,
  All marked with mute surmise
My radiance rare and fathomless,
When I came back from Lyonnesse
  With magic in my eyes!

Hardy's love poems, apart from the total emotional range which
they display—their intensity, tenderness, poignancy, delicacy,
wistfulness, originality—are also remarkable, as Carl Weber points
out, for providing a complete summary of his adult life; the poems
run the whole gamut, from first sight of the loved one through
courtship to marriage to quarrelling to staled familiarity, disillu-
sion, bitterness, division and death, and, thereafter, and most
remarkable of all, they plumb new depths of emotion in self-
examination, remorse, expiation and a rebirth of the original love.
Lyonnesse marks the start of the cycle; the next two poems
were all written in that inspired period 1912–13, when, following Emma's death, Hardy revisited the Boscastle area and was
overwhelmed by nostalgic memories of their early experiences
before the long intervening years of their unhappy and ill-assorted
marriage.

THOMAS HARDY
At Castle Boterel

As I drive to the junction of lane and highway,
　And the drizzle bedrenches the waggonette,
I look behind at the fading byway,
　　And see on its slope, now glistening wet,
　　　Distinctly yet

Myself and a girlish form benighted
　In dry March weather. We climb the road
Beside a chaise. We had just alighted
　　To ease the sturdy pony's load
　　　When he sighed and slowed.

What we did as we climbed, and what we talked of
　Matters not much, nor to what it led,—
Something that life will not be balked of
　　Without rude reason till hope is dead,
　　　And feeling fled.

It filled but a minute. But was there ever
　A time of such quality, since or before,
In that hill's story? To one mind never,
　　Though it has been climbed, foot-swift, foot-sore,
　　　By thousands more.

Primaeval rocks form the road's steep border,
　And much have they faced there, first and last,
Of the transitory in Earth's long order;
　　But what they record in colour and cast
　　　Is—that we two passed.

And to me, though Time's unflinching rigour,
　In mindless rote, has ruled from sight
The substance now, one phantom figure
　　Remains on the slope, as when that night
　　　Saw us alight.

I look and see it there, shrinking, shrinking,
　I look back at it amid the rain
For the very last time; for my soul is sinking,
　　And I shall traverse old love's domain
　　　Never again.

88

THOMAS HARDY
Beeny Cliff

O the opal and the sapphire of that wandering western sea,
And the woman riding high above with bright hair flapping
free—
The woman whom I loved so, and who loyally loved me.

The pale mews plained below us, and the waves seemed far
away
In a nether sky, engrossed in saying their ceaseless babbling
say,
As we laughed light-heartedly aloft on that clear-sunned
March day.

A little cloud then cloaked us, and there flew an irised rain,
And the Atlantic dyed its levels with a dull misfeatured
stain,
And then the sun burst out again, and purples prinked the
main.

—Still in all its chasmal beauty bulks old Beeny to the sky,
And shall she and I not go there once again now March is
nigh,
And the sweet things said in that March say anew there by
and by?

What if still in chasmal beauty looms that wild weird
western shore,
The woman now is—elsewhere—whom the ambling pony
bore,
And nor knows nor cares for Beeny, and will laugh there
nevermore.

I should like to have included two more of Hardy's "posthumous"
love poems, *The Going* and *The Voice*. However, both poems are
similar in structural shape and theme and, with space limitations
in mind, I have opted for *The Voice*. In the days following
Emma's death, one can imagine Hardy walking out at dusk from
Max Gate, the house built to his own architectural design on the
road a mile outside Dorchester, and, as he ponders the mystery of
Emma's death, feeling for a moment her spirit's presence before
being recalled by the autumnal evening to his rueful solitude.

THOMAS HARDY
The Voice

Woman much missed, how you call to me, call to me,
Saying that now you are not as you were
When you had changed from the one who was all to me,
But as at first, when our day was fair.

Can it be you that I hear? Let me view you, then,
Standing as when I drew near to the town
Where you would wait for me; yes, as I knew you then,
Even to the original air-blue gown!

Or is it only the breeze, in its listlessness
Travelling across the wet mead to me here,
You being ever dissolved to wan wistlessness,
Heard no more again far or near?

   Thus I; faltering forward,
   Leaves around me falling,
Wind oozing thin through the thorn from norward,
   And the woman calling.

ROBERT HERRICK
To the Virgins, Who Make Much of Time

Gather ye rosebuds while ye may,
   Old time is still a-flying:
And this same flower that smiles to-day
   To-morrow will be dying.

The glorious lamp of heaven, the sun,
   The higher he's a-getting,
The sooner will his race be run,
   And nearer he's to setting.

That age is best which is the first,
   When youth and blood are warmer;
But being spent, the worse, and worst
   Times still succeed the former.

Then be not coy, but use your time,
  And while ye may go marry:
For having lost but once your prime
  You may for ever tarry.

ANDREW MARVELL
To His Coy Mistress

Had we but world enough, and time,
This coyness, lady, were no crime.
We would sit down, and think which way
To walk, and pass our long love's day.
Thou by the Indian Ganges' side
Should'st rubies find: I by the tide
Of Humber would complain. I would
Love you ten years before the Flood,
And you should, if you please, refuse
Till the conversion of the Jews.
My vegetable love should grow
Vaster than empires, and more slow;
An hundred years should go to praise
Thine eyes, and on thy forehead gaze:
Two hundred to adore each breast:
But thirty thousand to the rest;
An age at least to every part,
And the last age should show your heart.
For, lady, you deserve this state,
Nor would I love at lower rate.
  But at my back I always hear
Time's wingèd chariot hurrying near:
And yonder all before us lie
Deserts of vast eternity.
Thy beauty shall no more be found;
Nor in thy marble vault, shall sound
My echoing song: then worms shall try
That long-preserved virginity,
And your quaint honour turn to dust,
And into ashes all my lust.
The grave's a fine and private place,
But none, I think, do there embrace.

Now, therefore, while the youthful hue
Sits on thy skin like morning dew,
And while thy willing soul transpires
At every pore with instant fires,
Now let us sport us while we may;
And now, like amorous birds of prey,
Rather at once our Time devour,
Than languish in his slow-chapt power.
Let us roll all our strength and all
Our sweetness up into one ball,
And tear our pleasures with rough strife
Thorough the iron gates of life.
Thus, though we cannot make our Sun
Stand still, yet we will make him run.

ROBERT HERRICK
Upon Julia's Clothes

Whenas in silks my Julia goes
Then, then (methinks) how sweetly flows
The liquefaction of her clothes.

Next, when I cast mine eyes and see
That brave vibration each way free;
O how that glittering taketh me!

Utilitarian and unisex though they may be, jeans allow of no "liquefaction," and the twentieth-century male suitor is thereby denied a delight enjoyed by his more fortunate forbears. Sir John Betjeman's subaltern, however, finds some compensation in being overwhelmed by his beloved on the tennis court.

SIR JOHN BETJEMAN
A Subaltern's Love-song

Miss J. Hunter Dunn, Miss J. Hunter Dunn,
Furnish'd and burnish'd by Aldershot sun,
What strenuous singles we played after tea,
We in the tournament—you against me!

Love-thirty, love-forty, oh! weakness of joy,
The speed of a swallow, the grace of a boy,
With carefullest carelessness, gaily you won,
I am weak from your loveliness, Joan Hunter Dunn.

Miss Joan Hunter Dunn, Miss Joan Hunter Dunn,
How mad I am, sad I am, glad that you won.
The warm-handled racket is back in its press,
But my shock-headed victor, she loves me no less.

Her father's euonymus shines as we walk,
And swing past the summer-house, buried in talk,
And cool the verandah that welcomes us in
To the six-o'clock news and a lime-juice and gin.

The scent of the conifers, sound of the bath,
The view from my bedroom of moss-dappled path,
As I struggle with double-end evening tie,
For we dance at the Golf Club, my victor and I.

On the floor of her bedroom lie blazer and shorts
And the cream-coloured walls are be-trophied with sports,
And westering, questioning settles the sun
On your low-leaded window, Miss Joan Hunter Dunn.

The Hillman is waiting, the light's in the hall,
The pictures of Egypt are bright on the wall,
My sweet, I am standing beside the oak stair
And there on the landing's the light on your hair.

By roads "not adopted", by woodlanded ways,
She drove to the club in the late summer haze,
Into nine-o'clock Camberley, heavy with bells
And mushroomy, pine-woody, evergreen smells.

Miss Joan Hunter Dunn, Miss Joan Hunter Dunn,
I can hear from the car-park the dance has begun.
Oh! full Surrey twilight! importunate band!
Oh! strongly adorable tennis-girl's hand!

Around us are Rovers and Austins afar,
Above us, the intimate roof of the car,
And here on my right is the girl of my choice,
With the tilt of her nose and the chime of her voice,

And the scent of her wrap, and the words never said,
And the ominous, ominous dancing ahead.
We sat in the car park till twenty to one
And now I'm engaged to Miss Joan Hunter Dunn.

PHILIP LARKIN
Lines on a Young Lady's Photograph Album

At last you yielded up the album, which,
Once open, sent me distracted. All your ages
Matt and glossy on the thick black pages!
Too much confectionery, too rich;
I choke on such nutritious images.

My swivel eye hungers from pose to pose—
In pigtails, clutching a reluctant cat;
Or furred yourself, a sweet girl-graduate;
Or lifting a heavy-headed rose
Beneath a trellis, or in a trilby hat

(Faintly disturbing, that, in several ways)—
From every side you strike at my control,
Not least through these disquieting chaps who loll
At ease about your earlier days:
Not quite your class, I'd say, dear, on the whole.

But, O photography! as no art is,
Faithful and disappointing! that records
Dull days as dull, and hold-it smiles as frauds,
And will not censor blemishes
Like washing-lines, and Hall's Distemper boards,

But shows the cat as disinclined, and shades
A chin as doubled when it is, what grace
Your candour thus confers upon her face!
How overwhelmingly persuades
That this is a real girl in a real place,

In every sense empirically true!
Or is it just the past? Those flowers, that gate,
Those misty parks and motors, lacerate
Simply by being over; you
Contract my heart by looking out of date.

94

Yes, true; but in the end, surely, we cry
Not only at exclusion, but because
It leaves us free to cry. We know what was
Won't call on us to justify
Our grief, however hard we yowl across

The gap from eye to page. So I am left
To mourn (without a chance of consequence)
You, balanced on a bike against a fence;
To wonder if you'd spot the theft
Of this one of you batting; to condense

In short, a past that no one now can share,
No matter whose your future; calm and dry,
It holds you like a haven, and you lie
Unvariably lovely there,
Smaller and clearer as the years go by.

Discussion topics

In their admirable textbook *The Practical Criticism of Poetry*, C. B. Cox and A. E. Dyson provide an excellent dialogue analysis of this poem and I am indebted to them for these questions:

a. Do you think the speaker in the poem is the poet in person or some figure in a dramatic monologue?

b. What evidence is there for assuming the speaker of the poem loved the girl in the past and missed (or refused) an opportunity to propose to her?

c. Does the speaker of the poem try to make his readers identify with him? If so, is he successful?

d. Explain as exactly as you can:
     (i)   "too much confectionery"
    (ii) "faintly disturbing, that, in several ways"
   (iii) "in every sense empirically true"
   (iv) "exclusion"
    (v) "the gap from eye to page"
   (vi) "unvariably lovely"

e. If you were looking for someone to read this poem aloud what kind of voice and mannerisms would be most appropriate? What, in fact, is the tone of the poem?

VII

SONG

Nursery rhymes and ballads are primitive poetic manifestations. Before the invention of printing most poetry and verse had necessarily to be passed from one generation to another by word of mouth. Rhyme and rhythm greatly aided the memorising process, as did musical accompaniment and repetitious refrains. Emerging, as they did, from a more barbaric past, the ballads are almost exclusively concerned with battles and sudden death, whether through natural or unnatural causes, with treachery and the tragedy of unrequited love. Most ballads tell their stories with stark economy of effort, yet with an occasional flash of vivid detail; they plunge directly into a tale and move at a brisk pace to the tragic end. Frequently a dour and macabre humour underlies the irony of the story.

Sir Patrick Spens exemplifies all these characteristics of the ballad and remains in addition a thrilling poem. In four quick opening lines we are immediately introduced to the setting, the tragic hero, and the problem. By liberal use of direct speech, whether by Sir Patrick Spens himself, or by one of his knights, or by the king, the story moves with sinister speed to its dramatic climax and ironic conclusion. The ballad is full of refrain-type phrases which the minstrel's audience would no doubt have repeated in harmony:

> "To Noroway, to Noroway,
>   To Noroway o'er the foam."
> "They hadna' sailed a league, a league,
>   A league but barely three."
> "O lang, lang may the ladies sit"
> "Half o'er, half o'er, to Aberdour"

Finally, the ironic humour carries an extraordinarily modern ring:

> "O laith, laith were the Scottish lords
>   To wet their cork-heeled schoon;
> But lang or ere the play was played,
>   They wet their hats aboon!"

To enjoy the ballad's full flavour it is essential to introduce a strong Scottish accent to the reading!

98

ANONYMOUS BALLAD
Sir Patrick Spens

The King sits in Dumferline town
  Drinking the blude-red wine;
"O whar will I get a guid sailor,
  To sail this ship of mine?"

Up and spak an eldern knicht,
  Sat at the king's richt knee;
"Sir Patrick Spens is the best sailor
  That ever sailed the sea."

The king has written a braid letter,
  And signed it wi' his hand;
And sent it to Sir Patrick Spens,
  Was walking on the strand.

"To Noroway, to Noroway,
  To Noroway o'er the foam;
The king's own daughter of Noroway,
  'Tis thou must bring her hame!"

The first line that Sir Patrick read
  A loud laugh laughed he;
The next line that Sir Patrick read
  The tear blinded his ee.

"O wha is this has done this deed,
  This ill deed done to me;
To send me out this time o' the year
  To sail upon the sea?

"Make haste, make haste, my merry men all,
  Our guid ship sails the morn."
"O say not so, my master dear,
  For I fear a deadly storm.

"I saw the new moon late yestere'en
  Wi' the auld moon in her arm;
And if we go to sea, master,
  I fear we'll come to harm."

They hadna' sailed a league, a league,
    A league, but barely three,
When the sky grew dark and the wind blew loud,
    And gurly grew the sea.

The anchor brake, the topmast split,
    'Twas sich a deadly storm,
The waves came over the broken ship
    Till a' her sides were torn.

O laith, laith were the Scottish lords
    To wet their cork-heeled schoon;
But lang or ere the play was played,
    They wet their hats aboon!

O lang, lang may the ladies sit
    Wi' their fans into their hand,
Or ere they see Sir Patrick Spens
    Come sailing to the strand.

O lang, lang may the ladies stand
    Wi' their gold kames in their hair,
Waiting for their ain dear lords,
    For them they'll see na mair.

Half o'er, half o'er, to Aberdour,
    'Tis fifty fathom deep.
'An there lies gude Sir Patrick Spens
    Wi' the Scots lords at his feet.

John Masefield's long narrative poems—*Reynard the Fox, Dauber, The Daffodil Fields, Right Royal, The Widow in the Bye Street*—are nowadays sadly neglected. I admire particularly *The Everlasting Mercy*, which includes, amongst many other excellent things, a wonderful description of a barefisted fight. Following his victory over Billy Myers, Saul Kane celebrates in a boozing session at the inn and this extract takes on from there. In a story of some fifteen hundred lines Masefield maintains an extraordinary melodic variety despite employing octosyllabic couplets which can so easily become monotonous.

JOHN MASEFIELD
Extract from *The Everlasting Mercy*

From three long hours of gin and smokes,
And two girls' breath and fifteen blokes',
A warmish night, and windows shut,
The room stank like a fox's gut.
The heat and smell and drinking deep
Began to stun the gang to sleep.
Some fell downstairs to sleep on the mat,
Some snored it sodden where they sat.
Dick Twot had lost a tooth and wept,
But all the drunken others slept.
Jane slept beside me in the chair,
And I got up; I wanted air.

I opened window wide and leaned
Out of that pigstye of the fiend
And felt a cool wind go like grace
About the sleeping market-place.
The clock struck three, and sweetly, slowly,
The bells chimed Holy, Holy, Holy;
And in a second's pause there fell
The cold note of the chapel bell,
And then a cock crew, flapping wings,
And summat made me think of things.
How long those clicking clocks had gone
From church and chapel, on and on,
Ticking the time out, ticking slow
To men and girls who'd come and go,
And how they ticked in belfry dark
When half the town was bishop's park,
And how they rung a chime full tilt
The night after the church was built,
And how that night was Lambert's Feast,
The night I'd fought and been a beast.
And how a change had come. And then
I thought, " You tick to different men."
What with the fight and what with drinking
And being awake alone there thinking,

My mind began to carp and tetter,
"If this life's all, the beasts are better."
And then I thought, "I wish I'd seen
The many towns this town has been;
I wish I knew if they'd a-got
A kind of summat we've a-not,
If them as built the church so fair
Were half the chaps folk say they were;
For they'd the skill to draw their plan,
And skill's a joy to any man;
And they'd the strength, not skill alone,
To build it beautiful in stone;
And strength and skill together thus . . .
O, they were happier men than us.

"But if they were, they had to die
The same as everyone and I
And no one lives again, but dies,
And all the bright goes out of eyes,
And all the skill goes out of hands,
And all the wise brain understands,
And all the beauty, all the power
Is cut down like a withered flower.
In all the show from birth to rest
I give the poor dumb cattle best."

I wondered, then, why life should be,
And what would be the end of me
When youth and health and strength were gone
And cold old age came creeping on?
A keeper's gun? The Union ward?
Or that new quod in Hereford?
And looking round I felt disgust
At all the nights of drink and lust,
And all the looks of all the swine
Who'd said that they were friends of mine;
And yet I know, when morning came,
The morning would be just the same,
For I'd have drinks and Jane would meet me
And drunken Silas Jones would greet me,

And I'd risk quod and keeper's gun
Till all the silly game was done.
"For parson chaps are mad supposin'
A chap can change the road he's chosen."

And then the Devil whispered, "Saul,
Whey should you want to live at all?
Why fret and sweat and try to mend?
It's all the same thing in the end.
But when it's done," he said, "it's ended.
Why stand it, since it can't be mended?"
And in my heart I heard him plain,
"Throw yourself down and end it, Kane."

"Why not?" said I. "Why not? But no.
I won't. I've never had my go.
I've not had all the world can give.
Death by and by, but first I'll live.
The world owes me my time of times,
And that time's coming now, by crimes."

A madness took me then. I felt
I'd like to hit the world a belt.
I felt that I could fly through air,
A screaming star with blazing hair,
A rushing comet, crackling, numbing
The folk with fear of judgment coming,
A 'Lijah in a fiery car
Coming to tell folk what they are.

"That's what I'll do," I shouted loud,
"I'll tell this sanctimonious crowd,
This town of window-peeping, prying,
Maligning, peering, hinting, lying,
Male and female human blots
Who would, but daren't be, whores and sots,
That they're so steeped in petty vice
That they're less excellent than lice,
That they're so soaked in petty virtue
That touching one of them will dirt you,

Dirt you with the stain of mean
Cheating trade and going between,
Pinching, starving, scraping, hoarding,
Spying through the chinks of boarding
To see if Sue the prentice lean
Dares to touch the margarine.
Fawning, cringing, oiling boots,
Raging in the crowd's pursuits,
Flinging stones at all the Stephens,
Standing firm with all the evens,
Making hell for all the odd,
All the lonely ones of God,
Those poor lonely ones who find
Dogs more mild than human kind.

. . . .

At that I tore my clothes in shreds
And hurled them on the window leads;
I flung my boots through both the winders
And knocked the glass to little flinders;
The punch bowl and the tumblers followed,
And then I seized the lamps and holloed,
And down the stairs, and tore back bolts,
As mad as twenty blooded colts;
And out into the street I pass,
As mad as two-year-olds at grass,
A naked madman waving grand
A blazing lamp in either hand.
I yelled like twenty drunken sailors,
"The devil's come among the tailors."
A blaze of flame behind me streamed,
And then I clashed the lamps and screamed,
"I'm Satan, newly come from hell."
And then I spied the fire-bell.

I've been a ringer, so I know
How best to make a big bell go.
So on to bell-rope swift I swoop,
And stick my one foot in the loop
And heave a down-swing till I groan,

"Awake, you swine, you devil's own."
I made the fire-bell awake,
I felt the bell-rope throb and shake;
I felt the air mingle and clang
And beat the walls a muffled bang,
And stifle back and boom and bay
Like muffled peals on Boxing Day,
And then surge up and gather shape,
And spread great pinions and escape;
And each great bird of clanging shrieks
O Fire! Fire! from iron beaks.

. . . .

Up go the winders, out come heads,
I heard the springs go creak in beds;
But still I heave and sweat and tire,
And still the clang goes "Fire! Fire!"
"Where is it, then? Who is it there?
You ringer stop, and tell us where."
"Run round and let the Captain know."
"It must be bad, he's ringing so."
"It's in the town, I see the flame;
Look there! Look there, how red it came."
"Where is it, then? O stop the bell."
I stopped and called: "It's fire of hell;
And this is Sodom and Gomorrah,
And now I'll burn you up, begorra."

. . . .

The men who don't know to the root
The joy of being swift of foot,
Have never known divine and fresh
The glory of the gift of flesh,
Nor felt the feet exult, nor gone
Along a dim road, on and on,
Knowing again the bursting glows
The mating hare in April knows,
Who tingles to the pads with mirth
At being the swiftest thing on earth.
O, if you want to know delight,
Run naked in an autumn night,

And laugh, as I laughed then, to find
A running rabble drop behind,
And whang, on every door you pass,
Two copper nozzles, tipped with brass,
And doubly whang at every turning,
And yell, "All hell's let loose, and burning."

I beat my brass and shouted fire
At doors of parson, lawyer, squire,
At all three doors I threshed and slammed
And yelled aloud that they were damned.
I clodded squire's glass with turves
Because he spring-gunned his preserves.
Through parson's glass my nozzle swishes
Because he stood for loaves and fishes,
But parson's glass I spared a tittle.
He give me an orange once when little,
And he who gives a child a treat
Makes joy-bells ring in Heaven's street,
And he who gives a child a home
Builds palaces in Kingdom come,
And she who gives a baby birth
Brings Saviour Christ again to Earth,
For life is joy, and mind is fruit,
And body's precious earth and root.
But lawyer's glass—well, never mind,
Th'old Adam's strong in me, I find.
God pardon man, and may God's son
Forgive the evil things I've done.

What more? By Dirty Lane I crept
Back to the "Lion," where I slept.
The raging madness hot and floodin'
Boiled itself out and left me sudden,
Left me worn out and sick and cold,
Aching as though I'd all grown old;
So there I lay, and there they found me
On door-mat, with a curtain round me.
Si took my heels and Jane my head
And laughed, and carried me to bed.

And from the neighbouring street they reskied
My boots and trousers, coat and weskit;
They bath-bricked both the nozzles bright
To be mementoes of the night,
And knowing what I should awake with
They flannelled me a quart to slake with,
And sat and shook till half-past two
Expecting Police Inspector Drew.

Saul Kane's escapade didn't end here. Next morning, after smashing up things at the Lion he ran out into the street again where he met the parson:

Old parson, red-eyed as a ferret
From nightly wrestlings with the spirit;
I ran across and barred his path.
His turkey gills went red as wrath
And then he froze, as parsons can.
"The police will deal with you, my man."
"Not yet," said I, "not yet they won't;
And now you'll hear me, like or don't."

And Saul gives the parson a piece of his mind for a further hundred hilarious lines.

Attempt to write at least twenty lines yourself (ten octosyllabic couplets) of Saul's diatribe!

SIR JOHN BETJEMAN
Extract from *Beside the Seaside*

Green Shutters, shut your shutters! Windyridge
Let winds unnoticed whistle round your hill!
High Dormers, draw your curtains! Slam the door,
And pack the family in the Morris eight.
Lock up the garage. Put her in reverse,
Back out with care, now, forward, off—away!
The richer people living farther out
O'ertake us in their Rovers. We, in turn,
Pass poorer families hurrying on foot
Towards the station. Very soon the town
Will echo to the groan of empty trams

And sweetshops advertise Ice Cream in vain.
Solihull, Headingley and Golders Green,
Preston and Swindon, Manchester and Leeds,
Braintree and Bocking, hear the sea! the sea!
The smack of breakers upon windy rocks,
Spray blowing backwards from their curling walls
Of green translucent water. England leaves
Her centre for her tide-line. Father's toes
Though now encased in coloured socks and shoes
And pressing the accelerator hard,
Ache for the feel of sand and little shrimps
To tickle in between them. Mother vows
To be more patient with the family:
Just for its sake she will be young again.
And, at that moment, Jennifer is sick
(Over-excitement must have brought it on,
The hurried breakfast and the early start)
And Michael's rather pale, and as for Anne . . .
"Please stop a moment, Hubert, anywhere."
        So evening sunlight shows us Sandy Cove
The same as last year and the year before.
Still on the brick front of the Baptist Church
SIX-THIRTY. PREACHER:—*Mr Pentecost*—
All visitors are welcomed. Still the quartz
Glitters along the tops of garden walls.
Those macrocarpa still survive the gales
They must have had last winter. Still the shops
Remain unaltered on the Esplanade—
The Circulating Library, the Stores,
Jill's Pantry, Cynthia's Ditty Box (Antiques),
Trecarrow (Maps and Souvenirs and Guides).
Still on the terrace of the big hotel
Pale pink hydrangeas turn a rusty brown
Where sea winds catch them, and yet do not die.
The bumpy lane between the tamarisks,
The escallonia hedge, and still it's there—
Our lodging-house, ten minutes from the shore.
Still unprepared to make a picnic lunch
Except by notice on the previous day.
Still nowhere for the children when it's wet

Except that smelly, overcrowded lounge.
And still no garage for the motor-car.
Still on the bedroom wall, the list of rules:
Don't waste the water. It is pumped by hand.
Don't throw old blades into the W.C.
Don't keep the bathroom long and don't be late
For meals and don't hang swim-suits out on sills
(A line has been provided at the back).
Don't empty children's sand-shoes in the hall.
Don't this, Don't that. Ah, still the same, the same
As it was last year and the year before—
But rather more expensive now, of course.
"Anne, Jennifer and Michael—run along
Down to the sands and find yourselves some friends
While Dad and I unpack." The sea! the sea!

    On a secluded corner of the beach
A game of rounders has been organised
By Mr. Pedder, schoolmaster and friend
Of boys and girls—particularly girls.
And here it was the tragedy began,
That life-long tragedy to Jennifer
Which ate into her soul and made her take
To secretarial work in later life
In a department of the Board of Trade.
See boys and girls assembled for the game.
Reflected in the rock pools, freckled legs
Hop, skip and jump in coltish ecstasy.
Ah! parted lips and little pearly teeth,
Wide eyes, snub noses, shorts, divided skirts!
And last year's queen of them was Jennifer.
The snubbiest, cheekiest, lissomest of all.
One smile from her sent Mr. Pedder back
Contented to his lodgings. She could wave
Her little finger and the elder boys
Came at her bidding. Even tiny Ruth,
Old Lady D'Erncourt's grandchild, pet of all,
Would bring her shells as timid offerings.
So now with Anne and Michael see her stand,
Our Jennifer, our own, our last year's queen.
For this year's début fully confident.

Oakham: Catmose Vale.

"Among the hills I sate
Alone, upon some jutting eminence
At the first hour of morning, when the Vale
Lay quiet in an utter solitude."

W. Wordsworth p.139

"Get in your places." Heard above the waves
Are Mr. Pedder's organising shouts.
"Come on. Look sharp. The tide is coming in!"
"He hasn't seen me yet," thinks Jennifer.
"Line up your team behind you, Christabel!"
On the wet sea-sand waiting to be seen
She stands with Anne and Michael. Let him turn
And then he'll see me. Let him only turn.
Smack went the tennis ball. The bare feet ran.
And smack again. "He's out! Well caught, Delphine!"
Shrieks, cartwheels, tumbling joyance of the waves.
Oh, Mr. Pedder, look! Oh here I am!
And there the three of them forlornly stood.
"You ask him, Jennifer." " No—Michael?—Anne?"
"I'd rather not." "Fains I." "It's up to you."
"Oh, very well, then." Timidly she goes,
Timid and proud, for the last time a child.
"Can we play, Mr. Pedder?" So he turns.
"*Who* have we here?" The jolly, jolly voice,
The same but not the same. "*Who* have we here?
The Rawlings children? Yes, of course you may,
Join that side, children, under Christabel."
No friendly wallop on the B.T.M.
No loving arm-squeeze and no special look.
Oh, darting heart-burn, *under Christabel*!
So all those holidays the bitter truth
Sank into Jennifer. No longer queen,
She had outgrown her strength, as Mummy said,
And Mummy made her wear these spectacles.
Because of Mummy she had lost her looks.
Had lost her looks? Still she was Jennifer.
The sands were still the same, the rocks the same,
The seaweed-waving pools, the bathing-cove,
The outline of the cliffs, the times of tide.
And I'm the same, of course I'm always ME.
But all that August those terrific waves
Thundered defeat along the rocky coast,
And ginger-beery surf hissed 'Christabel!'

W. H. Auden
Night Mail

(This poem was written as a commentary on a documentary film
produced by the Post Office.)

This is the Night Mail crossing the Border,
Bringing the cheque and the postal order,
Letters for the rich, letters for the poor,
The shop at the corner and the girl next door.
Pulling up Beattock, a steady climb—
The gradient's against her, but she's on time.

Past cotton-grass and moorland boulder,
Shovelling white steam over her shoulder,
Snorting noisily as she passes
Silent miles of wind-bent grasses.
Birds turn their heads as she approaches,
Stare from the bushes at her blank-faced coaches.
Sheep-dogs cannot turn her course;
They slumber on with paws across.
In the farm she passes no one wakes,
But a jug in the bedroom gently shakes.

Dawn freshens, the climb is done.
Down towards Glasgow she descends,
Towards the steam tugs yelping down the glade of cranes,
Towards the fields of apparatus, the furnaces
Set on the dark plain like gigantic chessmen.
All Scotland waits for her:
In dark glens, beside the pale-green lochs,
Men long for news

Letters of thanks, letters from banks,
Letters of joy from girl and boy,
Receipted bills and invitations
To inspect new stock or visit relations,
And applications for situations,
And timid lovers' declarations,
And gossip, gossip from all the nations,
News circumstantial, news financial,

Letters with holiday snaps to enlarge in,
Letters with faces scrawled in the margin,
Letters from uncles, cousins and aunts,
Letters to Scotland from the South of France,
Letters of condolence to Highlands and Lowlands,
Notes from overseas to Hebrides—
Written on paper of every hue,
The pink, the violet, the white and the blue,
The chatty, the catty, the boring, adoring,
The cold and official and the heart's outpouring,
Clever, stupid, short and long,
The typed and the printed and the spelt all wrong.

Thousands are still asleep,
Dreaming of terrifying monsters
Or a friendly tea beside the band at Cranston's or
    Crawford's:
Asleep in working Glasgow, asleep in well-set Edinburgh,
Asleep in granite Aberdeen.
They continue their dreams;
But shall wake soon and hope for letters,
And none will hear the postman's knock
Without a quickening of the heart,
For who can hear and feel himself forgotten?

Some years ago several school textbooks appeared which strongly advocated the chorus reading of poetry as a means to awaken appreciation. In my view, most poetry is murdered by group readings, but Auden's commentary does lend itself to such treatment since the sound and rhythmic effects can be enhanced by a variety of chorus accompaniment.

Quite apart from the ingenious way in which the poem captures the pulse and pace of a rail journey, the "North of the Border" excitement which grips the most unimaginative of passengers is rapidly conveyed in a few evocative phrases, whilst the journey, and the poem, are brought to a moving and satisfying conclusion by a sudden shift of interest from the general to the particular.

RUDYARD KIPLING
The 'Mary Gloucester'

I've paid for your sickest fancies; I've humoured your
    crackedest whim—
Dick, it's your daddy, dying; you've got to listen to him!
Good for a fortnight, am I? The doctor told you? He lied.
I shall go under by morning, and—Put that nurse outside.
'Never seen death yet, Dickie? Well, now is your time to
    learn,
And you'll wish you held my record before it comes to your
    turn.
Not counting the Line and the Foundry, the Yards and the
    village, too,
I've made myself and a million; but I'm damned if I made
    you.
Master at two-and-twenty, and married at twenty-three—
Ten thousand men on the pay-roll, and forty freighters at
    sea!
Fifty years between 'em, and every year of it fight,
And now I'm Sir Anthony Gloster, dying, a baronite:
For I lunched with his Royal 'Ighness—what was it the
    papers had?
'Not least of our merchant-princes.' Dickie, that's me, your
    dad!
I didn't begin with askings, *I* took my job and I stuck;
I took the chances they wouldn't, an' now they're calling
    it luck.
Lord, what boats I've handled—rotten and leaky and old—
Ran 'em, or—opened the bilge-cock, precisely as I was
    told.
Grub that 'ud bind you crazy, and crews that 'ud turn you
    grey,
And a big fat lump of insurance to cover the risk on the
    way.
The others they dursn't do it; they said they valued their life
(They've served me since as skippers). I went, and I
    took my wife.
Over the world I drove 'em, married at twenty-three,
And your mother saving the money and making a man of
    me.

I was content to be master, but she said there was better
    behind;
She took the chances I wouldn't, and I followed your
    mother blind.
She egged me to borrow the money, an' she helped me to
    clear the loan,
When we bought half-shares in a cheap 'un and hoisted
    a flag of our own.
Patching and coaling on credit, and living the Lord knew
    how,
We started the Red Ox freighters—we've eight-and-thirty
    now.
And those were the days of clippers, and the freights were
    clipper-freights,
And we knew we were making our fortune, but she died
    in Macassar Straits—
By the little Paternosters, as you come to the Union Bank—
And we dropped her in fourteen fathom; I pricked it off
    where she sank.
Owners we were, full owners, and the boat was christened
    for her,
And she died in the *Mary Gloster.* My heart, how young
    we were!

So I went on a spree round Java and wellnigh ran her
    ashore,
But your mother came and warned me and I wouldn't liquor
    no more;
Strict I stuck to my business, afraid to stop or I'd think,
Saving the money (she warned me), and letting the other
    men drink.
And I met M'Cullough in London (I'd saved five 'undred
    then),
And 'tween us we started the Foundry—three forges and
    twenty men.
Cheap repairs for the cheap 'uns. It paid, and the business
    grew;
For I bought me a steam-lathe patent, and that was a gold
    mine too.

'Cheaper to build 'em than buy 'em,' *I* said, but M'Cullough he shied,

And we wasted a year in talking before we moved to the Clyde.

And the Lines were all beginning, and we all of us started fair,

Building our engines like houses and staying the boilers square.

But M'Cullough 'e wanted cabins with marble and maple and all,

And Brussels an' Utrecht velvet, and baths and a Social Hall,

And pipes for closets all over, and cutting the frames too light,

But M'Cullough he died in the Sixties, and—well, I'm dying to-night . . .

I knew—I knew what was coming, when we bid on the *Byfleet*'s keel—

They piddled and piffled with iron. I'd given my orders for steel!

Steel and the first expansions. It paid, I tell you, it paid,

When we came with our nine-knot freighters and collared the long-run trade!

And they asked me how I did it, and I gave 'em the Scripture text,

"You keep your light so shining a little in front o' the next!"

They copied all they could follow, but they couldn't copy my mind,

And I left 'em sweating and stealing a year and a half behind.

Then came the armour-contracts, but that was M'Cullough's side;

He was always best in the Foundry, but better, perhaps, he died.

I went through his private papers; the notes was plainer than print;

And I'm no fool to finish if a man'll give me a hint.

(I remember his widow was angry.) So I saw what his drawings meant,

And I started the six-inch rollers, and it paid me sixty per
cent.
Sixty per cent with failures, and more than twice we could
do,
And a quarter-million to credit, and I saved it all for you!

I thought—it doesn't matter—you seemed to favour your
ma,
But you're nearer forty than thirty, and I know the kind
you are.
Harrer an' Trinity College! I ought to ha' sent you to
sea—
But I stood you an education, an' what have you done for
me?
The things I knew was proper you wouldn't thank me to
give,
And the things I knew was rotten you said was the way to
live.
For you meddled with books and pictures, an' china an'
etchin's an' fans,
And your rooms at college was beastly—more like a whore's
than a man's;
Till you married that thin-flanked woman, as white and as
stale as a bone,
An' she gave you your social nonsense; but where's that kid
o' your own?
I've seen your carriages blocking the half o' the Cromwell
Road,
But never the doctor's brougham to help the missus unload.
(So there isn't even a grandchild, an' the Gloster family's
done.)
Not like your mother, she isn't. *She* carried her freight
each run.
But they died, the pore little beggars! At sea she had 'em—
they died.
Only you, an' you stood it. You haven't stood much
beside.
Weak, a liar, and idle, and mean as a collier's whelp
Nosing for scraps in the galley. No help—my son was no
help!

So he gets three 'undred thousand, in trust and the
interest paid.
I wouldn't give it you, Dickie—you see, I made it in trade.
You're saved from soiling your fingers, and if you have no
child,
It all comes back to the business. 'Gad, won't your wife
be wild!
Calls and calls in her carriage, her 'andkerchief up to 'er eye:
"Daddy! dear Daddy's dyin'!" and doing her best to cry.
Grateful? Oh yes, I'm grateful, but keep her away from
here.
Your mother 'ud never ha' stood 'er, and, anyhow, women
are queer . . .
There's women will say I've married a second time. Not
quite!
But give pore Aggie a hundred, and tell her your lawyers'll
fight.
She was the best o' the boiling—you'll meet her before it
ends.
I'm in for a row with the mother—I'll leave you settle my
friends.
For a man he must go with a woman, which women don't
understand—
Or the sort that say they can see it they aren't the marrying
brand.

But I wanted to speak o' your mother that's Lady Gloster
still;
I'm going to up and see her, without its hurting the will.
Here! Take your hand off the bell-pull. Five thousand's
waiting for you,
If you'll only listen a minute, and do as I bid you do.
They'll try to prove me crazy, and, if you bungle, they
can;
And I've only you to trust to! (O God, why ain't it a
man?)
There's some waste money on marbles, the same as
M'Cullough tried—
Marbles and mausoleums—but I call that sinful pride.

There's some ship bodies for burial—we've carried 'em,
soldered and packed;
Down in their wills they wrote it, and nobody called *them*
cracked.
But me—I've too much money, and people might . . . All
my fault;
It come o' hoping for grandsons and buying that Wokin'
vault . . .
I'm sick o' the 'ole dam' business. I'm going back where I
came.
Dick, you're the son o' my body, and you'll take charge o'
the same!
I want to lie by your mother, ten thousand mile away,
And they'll want to send me to Woking; and that's where
you'll earn your pay.
I've thought it out on the quiet, the same as it ought to be
done—
Quiet, and decent, and proper—an' here's your orders, my
son.
You know the Line? You don't, though. You write to the
Board, and tell
Your father's death has upset you an' you're goin' to cruise
for a spell,
An' you'd like the *Mary Gloster*—I've held her ready for
this—
They'll put her in working order and you'll take her out
as she is.
Yes, it was money idle when I patched her and laid her
aside
(Thank God, I can pay for my fancies!)—the boat where
your mother died,
By the Little Paternosters, as you come to the Union
Bank,
We dropped her—I think I told you—and I pricked it off
where she sank.
(Tiny she looked on the grating—that oily, treacly sea—)
'Hundred and Eighteen East, remember, and South just
Three.
Easy bearings to carry—Three South—Three to the dot;
But I gave McAndrew a copy in case of dying—or not.

And so you'll write to McAndrew, he's Chief of the Maori
    Line;
They'll give him leave, if you ask 'em and say it's business
    o' mine.
I built three boats for the Maoris, an' very well pleased
    they were.
An' I've known Mac since the Fifties, and Mac knew me—
    and her.
After the first stroke warned me I sent him the money to
    keep
Against the time you'd claim it, committin' your dad to the
    deep;
For you are the son o' my body, and Mac was my oldest
    friend,
I've never asked 'im to dinner, but he'll see it out to the end.
Stiff-necked Glasgow beggar! I've heard he's prayed for my
    soul,
But he couldn't lie if you paid him, and he'd starve before
    he stole.
He'll take the *Mary* in ballast—you'll find her a lively ship;
And you'll take Sir Anthony Gloster, that goes on 'is
    wedding-trip,
Lashed in our old deck-cabin with all three port-holes wide,
The kick o' the screw beneath him and the round blue
    seas outside!
Sir Anthony Gloster's carriage—our 'ouse-flag flyin' free—
Ten thousand men on the pay-roll and forty freighters at
    sea!
He made himself and a million, but this world is a fleetin'
    show,
And he'll go to the wife of 'is bosom the same as he ought
    to go—
By the heel of the Paternosters—there isn't a chance to
    mistake—
And Mac'll pay you the money as soon as the bubbles
    break!
Five thousand for six weeks' cruising, the staunchest
    freighter afloat,
And Mac he'll give you your bonus the minute I'm out o'
    the boat!

He'll take you round to Macassar, and you'll come back
    alone;
He knows what I want o' the *Mary* . . . I'll do what I
    please with my own.
Your mother 'ud call it wasteful, but I've seven-and-thirty
    more;
I'll come in my private carriage and bid it wait at the
    door . . .
For my son 'e was never a credit; 'e muddled with books
    and art,
And 'e lived on Sir Anthony's money and 'e broke Sir
    Anthony's heart.
There isn't even a grandchild, and the Gloster family's
    done—
The only one you left me—O mother, the only one!
Harrer and Trinity College—me slavin' early an' late—
'An he thinks I'm dying crazy, and you're in Macassar Strait!
Flesh o' my flesh, my dearie, for ever an' ever amen,
That first stroke come for a warning. I ought to ha' gone
    to you then.
But—cheap repairs for a cheap 'un—the doctors said I'd do.
Mary, why didn't *you* warn me? I've allus heeded to you,
Excep'—I know—about women; but you are a spirit now;
An', wife, they was only women, and I was a man. That's
    how.
An' a man 'e must go with a woman, as you *could* not
    understand;
But I never talked 'em secrets. I paid 'em out o' hand.
Thank Gawd, I can pay for my fancies! Now what's five
    thousand to me,
For a berth off the Paternosters in the haven where I would
    be?
I believe in the Resurrection, if I read my Bible plain.
But I wouldn't trust 'em at Wokin'; we're safer at sea again.
For the heart it shall go with the treasure—go down to the
    sea in ships.
I'm sick of the hired women. I'll kiss my girl on her lips!
I'll be content with my fountain. I'll drink from my own well,
And the wife of my youth shall charm me—an' the rest can
    go to Hell!

(Dickie, he will, that's certain.) I'll lie in our standin' bed,
An' Mac'll take her in ballast—an' she trims best by the
    head . . .
Down by the head an' sinkin', her fires are drawn and cold,
And the water's splashin' hollow on the skin of the empty
    hold—
Churning an' choking and chuckling, quiet and scummy
    and dark—
Full to her lower hatches and risin' steady. Hark!
That was the after-bulkhead . . . She's flooded from stern to
    stern . . . .
'Never seen death yet, Dickie? . . . Well, now is your time
    to learn!

It has been said of Oscar Wilde that "he charmed his friends
out of criticism and irritated his enemies out of reason." Poet,
dramatist, essayist, critic, wit, aesthete, dandy, poseur, it was not
till his vicious two years' imprisonment, first at Wandsworth,
later at Reading, that Wilde experienced at first hand and in the
crudest possible form the horror and brutality of life reserved for
the castaways of Victorian society. Nowadays the mental malady
that caused Wilde's ruin is better understood by pathologists, and
the victimisation and social ostracism to which he was subjected
would no longer obtain. The experience hastened Wilde's death
at the untimely age of forty-six, but in the three years' freedom
which he enjoyed on his release, and which he spent as an exile
in France, he produced this moving ballad. G. K. Chesterton said
of it: "We hear a cry for common justice and brotherhood very
much deeper and more democratic . . . than anything the socialists
ever uttered in the boldest pages of Bernard Shaw." The ballad
is indeed a far cry from the intellectual romp and paradoxical
hilarity of *The Importance of Being Ernest*, which stands unique
in English drama as the supreme comedy of ridicule. At times
the ballad has lapses into bathos, but when one remembers the
sufferings out of which the poem was conceived such lapses are
surely excusable. On the whole, however, Wilde holds his emo-
tions under commendable control, and the ballad represents on
the one hand a damning indictment of the hypocritical nature of
Victorian society and on the other a poignant cry for the under-
privileged of every age.

OSCAR WILDE
Extracts from *The Ballad of Reading Gaol*

He did not wear his scarlet coat,
　For blood and wine are red,
And blood and wine were on his hands
　When they found him with the dead,
The poor dead woman whom he loved,
　And murdered in her bed.

He walked amongst the Trial Men
　In a suit of shabby grey;
A cricket cap was on his head,
　And his step seemed light and gay;
But I never saw a man who looked
　So wistfully at the day.

I never saw a man who looked
　With such a wistful eye
Upon that little tent of blue
　Which prisoners call the sky,
And at every drifting cloud that went
　With sails of silver by.

I walked with other souls in pain,
　Within another ring,
And was wondering if the man had done
　A great or little thing,
When a voice behind me whispered low,
　"That fellow's got to swing."

Six weeks our guardsman walked the yard,
　In the suit of shabby grey,
His cricket cap was on his head,
　And his step seemed light and gay,
But I never saw a man who looked
　So wistfully at the day.

I never saw a man who looked
　With such a wistful eye
Upon that little tent of blue
　Which prisoners call the sky,
And at every wandering cloud that trailed
　Its ravelled fleeces by.

He did not wring his hands nor weep,
   Nor did he peek or pine,
But he drank the air as though it held
   Some healthful anodyne;
With open mouth he drank the sun
   As though it had been wine!

And I and all the souls in pain,
   Who tramped the other ring,
Forgot if we ourselves had done
   A great or little thing,
And watched with gaze of dull amaze
   The man who had to swing.

And strange it was to see him pass
   With a step so light and gay,
And strange it was to see him look
   So wistfully at the day,
And strange it was to think that he
   Had such a debt to pay.

For oak and elm have pleasant leaves
   That in the spring-time shoot:
But grim to see is the gallows-tree
   With its adder-bitten root.
And, green or dry, a man must die
   Before it bears its fruit!

The loftiest place is that seat of grace
   For which all worldlings try:
But who would stand in hempen band
   Upon a scaffold high,
And through a murderer's collar take
   His last look at the sky?

It is sweet to dance to violins
   When Love and Life are fair:
To dance to flutes, to dance to lutes
   Is delicate and rare:
But it is not sweet with nimble feet
   To dance upon the air!

Burley-on-the-Hill, Rutland.
The apex of the "Burley Triangle" run where generations of Oak-
hamians have turned left and downhill for home.

"There were two good fellows I used to know,
– How distant it all appears!
We played together in football weather
And messed together for years."

J. K. Stephen p.143

So with curious eyes and sick surmise
  We watched him day by day,
And wondered if each one of us
  Would end the self-same way,
For none can tell to what red Hell
  His sightless soul may stray.

At last the dead man walked no more
  Amongst the Trial Men,
And I know that he was standing up
  In the black dock's dreadful pen,
And that never would I see his face
  In God's sweet world again.

Like two doomed ships that pass in storm
  We had crossed each other's way:
But we made no sign, we said no word,
  We had no word to say;
For we did not meet in the holy night,
  But in the shameful day.

A prison wall was round us both
  Two outcast men we were:
The world had thrust us from its heart,
  And God from out His care:
And the iron gin that waits for Sin
  Had caught us in its snare.

The Governor was strong upon
  The Regulations Act:
The Doctor said that Death was but
  A scientific fact:
And twice a day the chaplain called,
  And left a little tract.

And twice a day he smoked his pipe,
  And drank his quart of beer:
His soul was resolute, and held
  No hiding-place for fear:
He often said that he was glad
  The hangman's hands were near.

With slouch and swing around the ring
  We trod the Fool's Parade!
We did not care: we knew we were
  The Devil's Own Brigade:
And shaven head and feet of lead
  Made a merry masquerade.

We tore the tarry rope to shreds
  With blunt and bleeding nails;
We rubbed the doors, and scrubbed the floors,
  And cleaned the shining rails:
And, rank by rank, we soaped the plank,
  And clattered with the pails.

We sewed the sacks, we broke the stones,
  We turned the dusty drill:
We banged the tins, and bawled the hymns,
  And sweated on the mill:
But in the heart of every man
  Terror was lying still.

There is no chapel on the day
  On which they hang a man:
The Chaplain's heart is far too sick,
  Or his face is far too wan;
Or there is that written in his eyes
  Which none should look upon.

So they kept us close till nigh on noon,
  And then they rang the bell,
And the Warders with their jingling keys
  Opened each listening cell,
And down the iron stair we tramped,
  Each from his separate hell.

Out into God's sweet air we went
  But not in wonted way,
For this man's face was white with fear,
  And that man's face was grey,
And I never saw sad men who looked
  So wistfully at the day.

I never saw sad men who looked
   With such a wistful eye
Upon that little tent of blue
   We prisoners called the sky,
And at every careless cloud that passed
   In happy freedom by.

The warders strutted up and down
   And kept their herd of brutes,
Their uniforms were spick and span,
   And they wore their Sunday suits,
But we knew the work they had been at,
   By the quicklime on their boots.

For where a grave had opened wide,
   There was no grave at all:
Only a stretch of mud and sand
   By the hideous prison-wall,
And a little heap of burning lime,
   That the man should have his pall.

I know not whether Laws be right
   Or whether Laws be wrong;
All that we know who lie in gaol
   Is that the wall is strong;
And that each day is like a year,
   A year whose days are long.

With bars they blur the gracious moon,
   And blind the goodly sun:
And they do well to hide their Hell,
   For in it things are done
That Son of God nor son of Man
   Ever should look upon!

The vilest deeds, like poison weeds
   Bloom well in prison-air;
It is only what is good in Man
   That wastes and withers there:
Pale Anguish keeps the heavy gate,
   And the Warder is Despair.

In Reading gaol by Reading town
    There is a pit of shame,
And in it lies a wretched man
    Eaten by teeth of flame,
In a burning winding-sheet he lies,
    And his grave has got no name.

And there till Christ call forth the dead,
    In silence let him lie:
No need to waste the foolish tear,
    Or heave the windy sigh:
The man had killed the thing he loved,
    And so he had to die.

And all men kill the thing they love,
    By all let this be heard,
Some do it with a bitter look,
    Some with a flattering word,
The coward does it with a kiss,
    The brave man with a sword!

RUDYARD KIPLING
Danny Deever

'What are the bugles blowin' for?' said Files-on-Parade.
'To turn you out, to turn you out,' the Colour-Sergeant
    said,
'What makes you look so white, so white?' said Files-on-
    Parade.
'I'm dreadin' what I've got to watch,' the Colour-Sergeant
    said.
    For they're hangin' Danny Deever, you can hear the
        Dead March play,
    The Regiment's in 'ollow square—they're hangin' him
        to-day;
    They've taken of his buttons off an' cut his stripes away,
    An' they're hangin' Danny Deever in the mornin'.

'What makes the rear-rank breathe so 'ard?' said Files-on-
    Parade.
'It's bitter cold, it's bitter cold,' the Colour-Sergeant said.
'What makes that front-rank man fall down?' said Files-
    on-Parade.
'A touch o' sun, a touch o' sun,' the Colour-Sergeant said.
    They are hangin' Danny Deever, they are marchin' of
        'im round,
    They 'ave 'alted Danny Deever by 'is coffin on the
        ground:
    An' 'e'll swing in 'arf a minute for a sneakin' shootin'
        hound—
    O they're hangin' Danny Deever in the mornin'!

'Is cot was right- 'and cot to mine,' said Files-on-Parade,
'E's sleepin' out an' far to-night,' the Colour-Sergeant
    said.
'I've drunk 'is beer a score o' times,' said Files-on-Parade.
'E's drinking' bitter beer alone,' the Colour-Sergeant
    said.
    They are hangin' Danny Deever, you must mark 'im to
        'is place,
    For 'e shot a comrade sleepin'—you must look 'im in the
        face;
    Nine 'undred of 'is county an' the Regiment's disgrace,
    While they're hangin' Danny Deever in the mornin'.

'What's that so black agin the sun?' said Files-on-Parade.
'It's Danny fightin' 'ard for life,' the Colour-Sergeant said.
'What's that that whimpers over'ead?' said Files-on-Parade.
'It's Danny's soul that's passin' now,' the Colour-Sergeant
    said.
    For they're done with Danny Deever, you can 'ear the
        quickstep play,
    The Regiment's in column, an' they're marchin' us away:
    Ho! the young recruits are shakin', an' they'll want
        their beer to-day,
    After hangin' Danny Deever in the mornin'!

In 1941 T. S. Eliot surprised the critics by publishing a collection of Kipling's poetry with a highly laudatory preface by himself. As always with Eliot's criticism, he had much that was original to say not just about Kipling but about poetry in general. He thought that Kipling was above all else a "ballad-writer" who at times attained the intensity of poetry. "A ballad," wrote Eliot, "must have a meaning immediately apprehensible by its auditors. Repeated hearings may confirm the first impressions, may repeat the effect, but full understanding should be conveyed at one hearing . . . repetitions and refrains may contribute an incantatory effect."

Eliot went on to say that a ballad could be appreciated at two levels by two types of reader, the sophisticated and the half-educated. He thought that Kipling largely ignored the sophisticated reader and single-mindedly attempted to "convey no more to the simple-minded than can be taken in on one reading or hearing. (His ballads) are best when read aloud and the ear requires no training to follow them easily. With this simplicity of purpose goes a consummate gift of word, phrase, and rhythm. There is no poet who is less open to the charge of repeating himself. . . . The variety of form which Kipling manages to devise for his ballads is remarkable: each is distinct and perfectly fitted to the content and the mood which the poem has to convey. Nor is the versification too regular: there is the monotonous beat only when the monotonous is what is required; and the irregularities of scansion have a wide scope. One of the most interesting exercises in the combination of heavy beat and variation of pace is found in *Danny Deever*, a poem which is technically (as well as in content) remarkable. The regular recurrence of the same end-words, which gain immensely by imperfect rhyme ("parade" and "said") gives the feeling of marching feet and the movement of men in disciplined formation—in a unity of movement which enhances the horror of the occasion and the sickness which seizes the men as individuals; and the slightly quickened pace of the final lines marks the change in movement and in music. There is no single word or phrase which calls too much attention to itself, or which is not there for the sake of the total effect, so that when the climax comes—

'What's that that whimpers over'ead?' said Files-on-Parade,
'It's Danny's soul that's passin' now,' the Colour-Sergeant
said,

(the word "whimper" being exactly right) the atmosphere has been
prepared for a complete suspension of disbelief."

VIII

SCHOOL

CHARLES CAUSLEY
Timothy Winters

Timothy Winters comes to school
With eyes as wide as a football-pool,
Ears like bombs and teeth like splinters:
A blitz of a boy is Timothy Winters.

His belly is white, his neck is dark,
And his hair is an exclamation-mark.
His clothes are enough to scare a crow
And through his britches the blue winds blow.

When teacher talks he won't hear a word
And he shoots down dead the arithmetic-bird,
He licks the patterns off his plate,
And he's not even heard of the Welfare State.

Timothy Winters has bloody feet
And he lives in a house on Suez Street.
He sleeps in a sack on the kitchen floor
And they say there aren't boys like him any more.

Old Man Winters likes his beer
And his missus ran off with a bombardier,
Grandma sits in the grate with a gin
And Timothy's dosed with an aspirin.

The Welfare Worker lies awake
But the law's as tricky as a ten-foot snake,
So Timothy Winters drinks his cup
And slowly goes on growing up.

At Morning Prayers the Headmaster helves
For children less fortunate than ourselves,
And the loudest response in the room is when
Timothy Winters roars 'Amen!'

So come one angel, come on ten:
Timothy Winters says 'Amen
Amen amen amen amen.'
Timothy Winters, Lord.
                    Amen.

Timothy Winters seems to me to symbolise, amongst other things, the aggressive self-confidence of youth in this technological age. He may be uncouth, but he represents a decided break from the subservient "working-class" pupil of fifty years ago and inhabits an altogether different and, in some respects, more natural and confident world than the doom-ridden public-schoolboy of the same era (see the Betjeman extract on p. 135). He also represents in his person the significant change in the pupil/teacher relationship which has occurred over the same period, a rule of fear, reinforced by the rod, having been replaced by a more humane relationship based on a genuine respect. It is the unfortunate teacher who cannot command that respect who finds the classroom situation fraught with such difficulties to-day . . . and a Timothy Winters, in a subtle way, constitutes an ever-lurking challenge to such authority as he may succeed in exercising. The sinister danger for our country is that Timothy Winters "slowly goes on growing up."

I know of few poems written from the teacher's rather than the pupil's point of view in the classroom. Perhaps the situation demands so much of the teacher that he (or she) is left with insufficient energy to elaborate on his/her state of exhaustion! D. H. Lawrence, of course, was in his younger days a member of the great profession and, I suspect, an inspiring teacher in spite of his instinctive aversion to finding himself in authority.

D. H. LAWRENCE
Last Lesson of the Afternoon

When will the bell ring, and end this weariness?
How long have they tugged the leash, and strained apart
My pack of unruly hounds; I cannot start
Them again on a quarry of knowledge they hate to hunt,
I can haul them and urge them no more.

No more can I endure to bear the brunt
Of the books that lie out on the desks: a full three score
Of several insults of blotted pages and scrawl
Of slovenly work that they have offered me.
I am sick and tired more than any thrall
Upon the woodstacks working weariedly.

　And shall I take
The last dead fuel and heap it on my soul
Till I rouse my will like a fire to consume
Their dross of indifference, and burn the scroll
Of their insults in punishment?—I will not!
I will not waste myself to embers for them,
Not all for them shall the fires of my life be hot,
For myself a heap of ashes of weariness, till sleep
Shall have raked the embers clear: I will keep
Some of my strength for myself, for if I should sell
It all for them, I should hate them—
—I will sit and wait for the bell.

Sir John Betjeman
Extracts from *Summoned by Bells*

Doom! Shivering doom! Clutching a leather grip
Containing things for the first night of term—
House-slippers, sponge-bag, pyjamas, Common Prayer,
My health certificate, photographs of home
(Where were my bike, my playbox and my trunk?)—
I walked with strangers down the hill to school.
The town's first gaslights twinkled in the cold.
Deserted by the coaches, poorly served
By railway, Marlborough was a lonely place;
The old Bath Road, in chalky whiteness, raised
Occasional clouds of dust as motors passed.

　. . . . .
Doom! Shivering doom! Inexorable bells
To early school, to chapel, school again:
Compulsory constipation, hurried meals
Bulked out with Whipped Cream Walnuts from the town.
At first there was the dread of breaking rules—

"Betjeman, you know that new boys mustn't show
Their hair below the peak of college caps:
Stand still and have your face slapped." "Sorry, Jones."
The dread of beatings! Dread of being late!
And greatest dread of all, the dread of games!

. . . .

There was a building known as Upper School
(Abolished now, thank God, and all its ways),
An eighteen-fifty warehouse smelling strong
Of bat-oil, biscuits, sweat and rotten fruit.
The corporate life of which the bishop spoke,
At any rate among the junior boys,
Went on within its echoing whitewashed walls.
    Great were the ranks and privileges there:
Four captains ruled, selected for their brawn
And skill at games; and how we reverenced them!
Twelve friends they chose as brawny as themselves.
'Big Fire' we called them; lording it they sat
In huge arm-chairs beside the warming flames
Or played at indoor hockey in the space
Reserved for them. The rest of us would sit
Crowded on benches round another grate.
    Before the master came for evening prep
The captains entered at official pace
And, walking down the alley-ways of desks,
Beat on their bent lids with supple canes.
This was the sign for new boys to arise,
To pick up paper, apple-cores and darts
And fill huge baskets with the muck they found;
Then wiping hands upon grey handkerchiefs
And trousers, settle down to Latin prose.

. . . .

Our discontents and enmities arose
Somewhere about the seventh week of term:
The holidays too far off to count the days
Till our release, the weeks behind, a blank.
"Haven't you heard?" said D. C. Wilkinson.
"Angus is to be basketed to-night."
Why Angus . . . ? Never mind. The victim's found.
Perhaps he sported coloured socks too soon,

Braunston, Rutland

"To smell the thrilling-sweet and rotten
Unforgettable, unforgotten
River-smell"

Rupert Brooke p.193

Perhaps he smarmed his hair with scented oil,
Perhaps he was 'immoral' or a thief.
We did not mind the cause: for Angus now
The game was up. His friends deserted him,
And after his disgrace they'd stay away
For fear of being basketed themselves.
"*By* the boys, *for* the boys. The boys know best.
Leave it to them to pick the rotters out
With that rough justice decent schoolboys know."
And at the end of term the victim left—
Never to wear an old Marlburian tie.
   In quieter tones we asked in Hall that night
Neighbours to pass the marge; the piles of bread
Lay in uneaten slices with the jam.
Too thrilled to eat we raced across the court
Under the frosty stars to Upper School.
Elaborately easy at his desk
Sat Angus, glancing through The Autocar.
Fellows walked past him trying to make it look
As if they didn't know his coming fate,
Though the boy's body called "Unclean! Unclean!"
And all of us felt goody-goody-good,
Nice wholesome boys who never smiled at all.
At ten to seven 'Big Fire' came marching in
Unsmiling, while the captains stayed outside
(For this was 'unofficial'). Twelve to one:
What chance had Angus? They surrounded him,
Pulled off his coat and trousers, socks and shoes
And, wretched in his shirt, they hoisted him
Into the huge waste-paper basket; then
Poured ink and treacle on his head. With ropes
They strung the basket up among the beams,
And as he soared I only saw his eyes
Look through the slats at us who watched below.
Seven. "It's prep." They let the basket down
And Angus struggled out. "Left! Right! Left! Right!"
We stamped and called as, stained and pale, he strode
Down the long alley-way between the desks,
Holding his trousers, coat and pointed shoes.
"You're for it next," said H. J. Anderson.

138

"I'm not." "You are. I've heard." So all that term
And three terms afterwards I crept about,
Avoiding public gaze. I kept my books
Down in the basement where the boot-hole was
And by its fishtail gas-jet nursed my fear.

William Wordsworth was fortunate enough to attend Hawkshead
School as a dayboy and so, unlike Sir John Betjeman, successfully
avoided the miseries of a fashionable public school boarding
education. In *The Prelude*, that extraordinary analysis of his mind's
awakening, he makes it clear that school never for one moment
interrupted the full and relevant education which he experienced
outside school in his walks around his "darling Vale."

WILLIAM WORDSWORTH
Extracts from *The Prelude*

Thus daily were my sympathies enlarged,
And thus the common range of visible things
Grew dear to me: already I began
To love the sun, a Boy I lov'd the sun,
Not as I since have lov'd him, as a pledge
And surety of our earthly life, a light
Which while we view we feel we are alive;
But, for this cause, that I had seen him lay
His beauty on the morning hills, had seen
The western mountain touch his setting orb,
In many a thoughtless hour, when, from excess
Of happiness, my blood appear'd to flow
With its own pleasure, and I breath'd with joy.
And from like feelings, humble though intense,
To patriotic and domestic love
Analogous, the moon to me was dear;
For I would dream away my purposes,
Standing to look upon her while she hung
Midway between the hills, as if she knew
No other region; but belong'd to thee,
Yea, appertain'd by a peculiar right
To thee and thy grey huts, my darling Vale!

. . . .

My morning walks
Were early; oft, before the hours of School
I travell'd round our little Lake, five miles
Of pleasant wandering, happy time!

  . . . .

Nor seldom did I lift our cottage latch
Far earlier, and before the vernal thrush
Was audible, among the hills I sate
Alone, upon some jutting eminence
At the first hour of morning, when the Vale
Lay quiet in an utter solitude.
How shall I trace the history, where seek
The origin of what I then have felt?
Oft in these moments such a holy calm
Did overspread my soul, that I forgot
That I had bodily eyes, and what I saw
Appear'd like something in myself, a dream,
A prospect in my mind.
    'Twere long to tell
What spring and autumn, what the winter snows,
And what the summer shade, what day and night,
The evening and the morning, what my dreams
And what my waking thoughts supplied, to nurse
That spirit of religious love in which
I walked with Nature. But let this, at least
Be not forgotten, that I still retain'd
My first creative sensibility,
That by the regular action of the world
My soul was unsubdu'd. A plastic power
Abode with me, a forming hand, at times
Rebellious, acting in a devious mood,
A local spirit of its own, at war
With general tendency, but for the most
Subservient strictly to the external things
With which it commun'd. An auxiliar light
Came from my mind which on the setting sun
Bestow'd new splendour, the melodious birds,
The gentle breezes, fountains that ran on,
Murmuring so sweetly in themselves, obey'd
A like dominion; and the midnight storm

Grew darker in the presence of my eye.
Hence my obeisance, my devotion hence,
And hence my transport.

What magical hours of walks or meditations Wordsworth enjoyed before school, hours which were not Betjeman's to command
at his regimented Marlborough. Hopefully, recent years have at
long last witnessed an awakening to true education at most boarding schools and the opportunity to savour the sun on the morning or evening hills and to "walk with Nature" outside the school
environment is at long last a recognized area of the curriculum.

C. Day Lewis
Walking Away

It is eighteen years ago, almost to the day—
A sunny day with the leaves just turning,
The touch-lines new-ruled—since I watched you play
Your first game of football, then, like a satellite
Wrenched from its orbit, go drifting away

Behind a scatter of boys. I can see
You walking away from me towards the school
With the pathos of a half-fledged thing set free
Into a wilderness, the gait of one
Who finds no path where the path should be.

That hesitant figure, eddying away
Like a winged seed loosened from its parent stem,
Has something I never quite grasp to convey
About nature's give-and-take—the small, the scorching
Ordeals which fire one's irresolute clay.

I have had worse partings, but none that so
Gnaws at my mind still. Perhaps it is roughly
Saying what God alone could perfectly show—
How selfhood begins with a walking away,
And love is proved in the letting go.

This poem was written for his son, Sean, a Shirburnian, like his father, and I have always wondered whether the setting for the poem is Sherborne itself. Part of what Day Lewis is trying to express is summed up by the French (who so often have an apt word for it)—"Partir, c'est un peu mourir."

Most readers will know of Lawrence's poetry through his very free-verse animal poems—*Snake*, *Kangaroo*, *Baby Tortoise*, and *Man and Bat* being all excellent poems for the classroom. But, when he chose, Lawrence could handle a tight rhythm and rhyme most effectively as he displays in this piece of cynical writing about Nottingham University. Since the university was only of college status in Lawrence's time (1906–8), I suspect again, perhaps unfairly, that Lawrence enjoyed working off his envy in this way upon the full university students who succeeded him!

D. H. LAWRENCE
Nottingham's New University

In Nottingham that dismal town
where I went to school and college,
they've built a new university
for a new dispensation of knowledge.

Built it most grand and cakily
out of the noble loot
derived from shrewd cash-chemistry
by good Sir Jesse Boot.

Little I thought when I was a lad
and turned my honest penny
over on Boot's Cash-Chemist's counter,
that Jesse, by turning many

Millions of similar honest pence
over, would make a pile
that would rise at last and blossom out
in grand and cakey style

Into a university
where smart men would dispense
doses of smart cash-chemistry
in language of common-sense!

That future Nottingham lads would be
cash-chemically B.Sc.
that Nottingham lights would rise and say:
—By Boots I am M.A.

From this I learn, though I knew it before
that culture has her roots
in the deep dung of cash, and love
is a last offshoot of Boots.

I came upon the following in a delightful anthology produced
in 1941 by the famous golf correspondent of *The Times* and
Country Life, Bernard Darwin. J. K. Stephen, the author, was
prompted to write in 1891 on "accidentally finding an old copy
of Stapylton's Eton School Lists." In his preface Darwin admitted that much of the verse in his anthology did not pretend
to vie with "poetry of lofty imagination" but, for all that, he
could never read Stephen's poem unmoved, and he added: "What
is called light verse can have very real feeling and its laughter
comes often near to tears."

J. K. STEPHEN
The Old School List

In a wild moraine of forgotten books,
  On the glacier of years gone by,
As I plied my rake for order's sake,
  There was one that caught my eye;
And I sat by the shelf till I lost myself,
  And roamed in a crowded mist,
And heard lost voices and saw lost looks,
  As I pored on an old School List.

What a jumble of names! there were some that I knew
  As a brother is known: to-day
Gone I know not where, nay I hardly care,
  For their places are full: and, they—
What climes they have ranged: how much they're changed!
  Time, place and pursuits assist
In transforming them: stay where you are: adieu!
  You are all in the old School List.

There are some who did nothing at school, much since;
    And others much then, since naught:
There are middle-aged men, grown bald since then:
    Some have travelled, and some have fought:
And some have written, and some are bitten
    With strange new faiths: desist
From tracking them; broker, or priest or prince,
    They are all in the old School List.

There's a grave grey lawyer in King's Bench Walk,
    Whose clients are passing few:
He seldom speaks: in those lonely weeks,
    What on earth can he find to do?
Well he stroked the eight—what a splendid fate!—
    And the Newcastle barely missed:
'A future Lord Chancellor!' so we'd talk
    In the days of the old School List.

There were several duffers and several bores,
    Whose faces I've half forgot,
Whom I live among, when the world was young,
    And who talked 'no end of rot':
Are they now little clerks who stroll in the Parks
    Or scribble with grimy fist;
Or rich little peers who hire Scotch moors?
    Well—they're all in the old School List.

There were some who were certain to prosper and thrive,
    And certain to do no more,
Who were 'capital chaps', and, tho' moderate saps,
    Would never stay in after four:
Now day after day they are packed away,
    After being connubially kissed,
To work in the city from ten to five:
    There they are in the old School List.

There were two good fellows I used to know,
    —How distant it all appears!
We played together in football weather,
    And messed together for years:
Now one of them's wed, and the other's dead
    So long that he's hardly missed
Save by us, who messed with him years ago:
    But we're all in the old School List.

IX

WAR

To those of us born between 1914–18 the impact of World War I hung heavy over our upbringing. As one whose father had mercifully survived four years as an infantry officer on the Western Front, the immediate aftermath of the war was heightened both through the immediate insight into the holocaust which his personal account of trench warfare provided and also through the series of outstanding books which poured from the publishers in the 1920s. I think, particularly, of E. M. Romarque's *All Quiet on the Western Front*, Robert Graves' *Goodbye to All That*, Edmund Blunden's *Undertones of War*, Frederick Manning's *Her Privates We*, Ernest Hemingway's *A Farewell to Arms*, and Siegfried Sassoon's trilogy, *Memoirs of a Fox-Hunting Man*, *Memoirs of an Infantry Officer*, and *Sherston's Progress*. All these were firsthand accounts by men of exceptional sensitivity and imagination who had supped full of the horrors of war and yet survived to write in compassionate, if cynical, mood about their firsthand experiences. To the youth of the twenties they were the equivalent of science fiction. Sassoon's work in particular affected me deeply and also provided, as it happened, an invaluable psychological preparation for the next war which, as the thirties sped by, loomed ever more inevitably and ominously. Graves, Blunden, and Sassoon himself were, of course, poets also, and initially it was Sassoon, even more than Wilfred Owen, who launched the realistic and embittered reaction to the earlier patriotic outpourings of Rupert Brooke.

If I should die, think only this of me,
That there's some corner of a foreign field
That is for ever England.

Now God be thanked Who has matched us with this
  hour,
And caught our youth, and wakened us from sleeping.

Brooke, actually, had only been faithfully reflecting the mood of a Britain resorting to arms after a century of peace, and it took the senseless mass-slaughter of the Somme in 1916, followed by the appalling miseries of Passchendaele in 1917, finally to quash this outburst of emotional patriotism. It was the front-line soldiers themselves who reacted first, chiefly against the cushioned staff officers and bigoted generals who were leading them to perdition, and ultimately against the hypocritical industrialists at home who were reaping fat fortunes out of armaments. Sassoon's *Base Details* is typical:

> If I were fierce and bald and short of breath,
>   I'd live with Scarlet Majors at the Base,
> And speed glum heroes up the line to death.
>   You'd see me with my puffy petulant face,
> Guzzling and gulping in the best hotel,
>   Reading the Roll of Honour. "Poor young chap,"
> I'd say—"I used to know his father well;
>   Yes, we've lost heavily in this last scrap."
> And when the war is done and youth stone dead,
>   I'd toddle safely home and die—in bed.

If the poetry of Blunden, Graves, Thomas, Owen, Sorley, and Sassoon gains much of its depth and power because it was struck upon the anvil of firsthand battle experience, is this to invalidate all war poetry written by non-combatants? Simply to postulate such a view is to expose its absurdity. No author can hope to write entirely from within his range of experience, and it is inevitable that some areas of his work will necessarily be apprehended only by his imagination working upon his experience. Lord David Cecil, speaking about Hardy as a novelist, makes a valid point about this when he says, "In any one artist only some aspects of his experience fertilise his imagination, strike sufficiently deep down into the fundamentals of his personality to kindle his creative spark." Perhaps the outstanding characteristic of Shakespeare's genius is that virtually all his experience seemed to "fertilise his imagination" so that his creative spark was kindled by an astonishing variety of human situations and characters, from ancient Rome to the Forest of Arden, from Lady Macbeth to Cordelia, or King Lear to Justice Shallow. So, in considering the war poetry of a non-combatant we have to ask ourselves if the incident about which he is moved to write—*The Charge of the Light Brigade*, *The Siege of Harfleur*, *The Burial of Sir John Moore after Corunna*—has really "struck sufficiently deep down into the fundamentals of his personality to kindle his creative spark." For myself, I am dubious about Tennyson's *Light Brigade* but happier about his *Ode on the Death of the Duke of Wellington*, although this is, of course, no war poem but a funereal dirge about warfare in which Tennyson captures magnificently the authentic organ tones of a solemn requiem. Shakespeare, as ever, ranges the whole field of human endeavour in war with equal assurance whether it be the king's clarion call to arms, the heat and burden of battle itself, sentry-go duties at night, or the front-line soldier's exasperation with his insufferable staff-officers. Kipling, although he has all the jargon of the soldier's trade at his finger-tips, lapses too easily into patriotic drum-beating or an embarrassing form of muscular Christianity between man and man, although his *Danny Deever*, as we have already seen, sounds an altogether different and compelling note of poignant mystery.

I must leave the reader to form his own judgment about Charles Wolfe's *Burial of Sir John Moore*. Because it was the first poem that my preparatory school ever required me to get by heart, it carries personal emotional overtones quite apart from those which it sounds for itself. But I think my English master knew what he was about when he decided that this poem should serve an eight-year-old as his introduction to poetry! Normally one would expect that, by mixing so many anapaests of triple time with a duple iambic rhythm, the poem would gather too much pace and vitality, e.g. Browning's

> I sprang to the stirrup and Joris, and he;
> I galloped, Dirck galloped, we galloped, all three.

but this doesn't happen in *The Burial*. Instead the anapaests serve to accentuate the mystery, tension, and sense of urgency—the need to bury the beloved general with all decency before taking to the boats. It even seems to me that the rhythm conveys some sense of the waves, which were to carry the mourners to safety, lapping at the Spanish shore.

CHARLES WOLFE
The Burial of Sir John Moore after Corunna

Not a drum was heard, not a funeral note,
  As his corse to the rampart we hurried;
Not a soldier discharged his farewell shot
  O'er the grave where our hero we buried.

We buried him darkly at dead of night,
  The sods with our bayonets turning,
By the struggling moonbeam's misty light
  And the lanthorn dimly burning.

No useless coffin enclosed his breast,
  Not in sheet or in shroud we wound him;
But he lay like a warrior taking his rest
  With his martial cloak around him.

Few and short were the prayers we said,
  And we spoke not a word of sorrow;
But we steadfastly gazed on the face that was dead,
  And we bitterly thought of the morrow.

We thought, as we hollowed his narrow bed,
  And smoothed down his lonely pillow,
That the foe and the stranger would tread o'er his head,
  And we far away on the billow!

Lightly they'll talk of the spirit that's gone,
  And o'er his cold ashes upbraid him—
But little he'll reck, if they let him sleep on
  In the grave where a Briton has laid him.

But half of our heavy task was done
  When the clock struck the hour for retiring;
And we heard the distant and random gun
  That the foe was solemnly firing.

Slowly and sadly we laid him down,
  From the field of his fame fresh and gory;
We carved not a line, and we raised not a stone,
  But we left him alone with his glory.

Truth compels me to add that men from the 9th Regiment of
Foot (the East Norfolk Regiment) dug the general's grave—not,

one presumes, with their bayonets!—and that it was eight o'clock in the morning before Moore's body was lowered into the grave by the red sashes of his staff and the chaplain read a few brief prayers at the graveside, "his voice scarcely audible above the rushing of the wind, the leaves of the prayerbook fluttering beneath his fingers" (Christopher Hibbert, *Corunna*). However, the battle itself, on the evening before, had certainly been fought in a confusing mist which hung about into the night, and it was the renewal of the sound of the "random gun" from the "sullen" enemy beyond the Heights of Santa Margarita which impressed haste upon Moore's staff. One must allow Charles Wolfe his poetic licence before assessing whether Moore's tragic and heroic death "struck sufficiently deep down into the fundamentals of his personality to kindle his creative spark."

Michael Drayton's *Agincourt* was another early preparatory school poem. Its dominant, upstanding rhythm, with the fourth short line and its inverted stresses ($-\smile\smile$ or $-\smile$ in place of the basic $\smile-$ iambic metre of the poem as a whole) acts as a sort of signature tune and imparts to the poem a buoyant, invigorating, aggressive quality all its own.

MICHAEL DRAYTON
Agincourt

Fair stood the wind for France
When we our sails advance,
Nor now to prove our chance
    Longer will tarry;
But putting to the main,
At Caux, the mouth of Seine,
With all his martial train
    Landed King Harry.

And taking many a fort,
Furnished in warlike sort,
Marcheth towards Agincourt
    In happy hour;
Skirmishing day by day
With those that stopped his way,
Where the French general lay
    With all his power.

Which, in his height of pride,
King Henry to deride,
His ransom to provide
 Unto him sending;
Which he neglects the while
As from a nation vile,
Yet with an angry smile
 Their fall portending.

And turning to his men,
Quoth our brave Henry then,
'Though they be one to ten
 Be not amazéd:
Yet have we well begun;
Battles so bravely won
Have ever to the sun
 By fame been raiséd.

'And for myself (quoth he)
This my full rest shall be:
England ne'er mourn for me
 Nor more esteem me:
Victor I will remain
Or on this earth lie slain,
Never shall she sustain
 Loss to redeem me.

'Poitiers and Cressy tell,
When most their pride did swell,
Under our swords they fell:
 No less our skill is
Than when our grandsire great,
Claiming the regal seat,
By many a warlike feat
 Lopped the French lilies.

The Duke of York so dread
The eager vaward led;
With the main Henry sped
 Among his henchmen.

Exeter had the rear,
A braver man not there:
O Lord, how hot they were
  On the false Frenchmen!

They now to fight are gone,
Armour on armour shone,
Drum now to drum did groan,
  To hear was wonder.
That with the cries they make
The very earth did shake:
Trumpet to trumpet spake,
  Thunder to thunder.

Well it thine age became,
O noble Erpingham,
Which didst the signal aim
  To our hid forces!
When from a meadow by,
Like a storm suddenly
The English archery
  Struck the French horses.

With Spanish yew so strong,
Arrows a cloth-yard long
That like to serpents stung,
  Piercing the weather;
None from his fellow starts,
But playing manly parts,
And like true English hearts
  Stuck close together.

When down their bows they threw,
And forth their bilbos drew,
And on the French they flew,
  Not one was tardy;
Arms were from shoulders sent,
Scalps to the teeth were rent,
Down the French peasants went—
  Our men were hardy.

This while our noble king,
His broadsword brandishing,
Down the French host did ding
    As to o'er whelm it;
And many a deep wound lent,
His arms with blood besprent,
And many a cruel dent
    Bruiséd his helmet.

Gloster, that duke so good,
Next of the royal blood,
For famous England stood
    With his brave brother;
Clarence, in steel so bright,
Though but a maiden knight,
Yet in that furious fight
    Scarce such another.

Warwick in blood did wade,
Oxford the foe invade,
And cruel slaughter made
    Still as they ran up;
Suffolk his axe did ply,
Beaumont and Willoughby
Bare them right doughtily,
    Ferrers and Fanhope.

Upon Saint Crispin's Day
Fought was this noble fray,
Which fame did not delay
    To England to carry.
O when shall English men
With such acts fill a pen?
Or England breed again
    Such a King Harry?

WILLIAM SHAKESPEARE
Henry V (Chorus to Act IV)

Now entertain conjecture of a time
When creeping murmur and the poring dark
Fills the wide vessel of the universe.
From camp to camp, through the foul womb of night,
The hum of either army stilly sounds,
That the fix'd sentinels almost receive
The secret whispers of each other's watch:
Fire answers fire; and through their paly flames
Each battle sees the other's umber'd face:
Steed threatens steed, in high and boastful neighs
Piercing the night's dull ear; and from the tents,
The armourers, accomplishing the knights,
With busy hammers closing rivets up,
Give dreadful note of preparation:
The country cocks do crow, the clocks do toll,
And the third hour of drowsy morning name.
Proud of their numbers and secure in soul,
The confident and over-lusty French
Do the low-rated English play at dice;
And chide the cripple tardy-gaited night,
Who, like a foul and ugly witch, doth limp
So tediously away. The poor condemnéd English,
Like sacrifices, by their watchful fires
Sit patiently, and inly ruminate
The morning's danger; and their gesture sad
Investing lank-lean cheeks, and war-worn coats,
Presenteth them unto the gazing moon
So many horrid ghosts. O, now, who will behold
The royal captain of this ruin'd band
Walking from watch to watch, from tent to tent,
Let him cry, 'Praise and glory on his head!'
For forth he goes and visits all his host;
Bids them good morrow with a modest smile,
And calls them brothers, friends, and countrymen.
Upon his royal face there is no note
How dread an army hath enrounded him;
Nor doth he dedicate one jot of colour
Unto the weary and all-watchéd night;

But freshly looks, and over-bears attaint
With cheerful semblance and sweet majesty;
That every wretch, pining and pale before,
Beholding him, plucks comfort from his looks:
A largess universal, like the sun,
His liberal eye doth give to every one,
Thawing cold fear. Then, mean and gentle all,
Behold, as may unworthiness define,
A little touch of Harry in the night.

I find it difficult to believe that Shakespeare didn't at some time in his life stand-to as a soldier at dawn! As always, he uses a wealth of homely imagery to reinforce his theme and give it a universal validity.

Discussion topics

a. Which illustrations do you think are particularly effective in the context of the situation?

b. Define as precisely as possible the objective meaning and the subjective connotations of the following words or phrases in italics: the *poring* dark, the *foul womb* of night, *dreadful* note of preparation, the *over-lusty* French, the *cripple tardy-gaited* night, like *sacrifices*, he *dedicate* one jot of colour, his *liberal* eye.

RICHARD LOVELACE
To Lucasta, Going to the Wars

Tell me not, Sweet, I am unkind,
    That from the nunnery
Of thy chaste breast and quiet mind
    To war and arms I fly.

True, a new mistress now I chase,
    The first foe in the field;
And with a stronger faith embrace
    A sword, a horse, a shield.

Yet this inconstancy is such
    As thou too shalt adore;
I could not love thee, Dear, so much,
    Loved I not Honour more.

Perfectly said, "*multum in parvo*," and anticipating the aphoristic skills of Alexander Pope by half a century.

WILLIAM SHAKESPEARE
Henry V (Act IV Scene iii)
Before Agincourt

I am indebted to D. H. Rylands for this note in his *Ages of Man*:
"Shakespeare learned his patriotism and foreign policy from Holinshed
and the other old chroniclers who followed in the train of that prince
of sporting-writers, Froissart. They treated warfare as we treat football
—as a spectacular, exciting, and fundamentally good-natured pastime,
arising from no particular causes except the love of competition and
productive of no consequences except the glory of the successful
athlete. King Henry's speech before Agincourt is the high-water mark
of football oratory."

If we are marked to die, we are enow
To do our country loss; and if to live,
The fewer men, the greater share of honour.
God's will! I pray thee, wish not one man more.
By Jove, I am not covetous for gold;
Nor care I who doth feed upon my cost;
It yearns me not if men my garments wear;
Such outward things dwell not in my desires:
But if it be a sin to covet honour,
I am the most offending soul alive.
No, faith, my coz, wish not a man from England:
God's peace! I would not lose so great an honour,
As one man more, methinks, would share from me,
For the best hope I have. O, do not wish one more!
Rather, proclaim it, Westmoreland, through my host,
That he which hath no stomach to this fight,
Let him depart; his passport shall be made,
And crowns for convoy put into his purse:
We would not die in that man's company
That fears his fellowship to die with us.
This day is called the feast of Crispian:
He that outlives this day, and comes safe home,
Will stand a tip-toe when this day is named,
And rouse him at the name of Crispian.
He that shall live this day, and see old age,
Will yearly on the vigil feast his neighbours,
And say, 'To-morrow is Saint Crispian':

Then will he strip his sleeve and show his scars,
And say, 'These wounds I had on Crispin's day.'
Old men forget; yet all shall be forgot,
But he'll remember with advantages
What feats he did that day: then shall our names,
Familiar in their mouths as household words,—
Harry the King, Bedford and Exeter,
Warwick and Talbot, Salisbury and Gloster,—
Be in their flowing cups freshly remembered.
This story shall the good man teach his son;
And Crispin Crispian shall ne'er go by,
From this day to the ending of the world,
But we in it shall be remembered,—
We few, we happy few, we band of brothers;
For he to-day that sheds his blood with me
Shall be my brother; be he ne'er so vile,
This day shall gentle his condition:
And gentlemen in England now a-bed
Shall think themselves accurst they were not here;
And hold their manhoods cheap whiles any speaks
That fought with us upon Saint Crispin's day.

ROBERT BROWNING
Home Thoughts, from the Sea

Nobly, nobly Cape Saint Vincent to the North-west died
    away;
Sunset ran, one glorious blood-red, reeking into Cadiz Bay;
Bluish 'mid the burning water, full in face Trafalgar lay;
In the dimmest North-east distance dawn'd Gibralter grand
    and gray;
'Here and here did England help me: how can I help
    England?'—say,
Whoso turns as I, this evening, turn to God to praise and
    pray,
While Jove's planet rises yonder, silent over Africa.

ALFRED TENNYSON
Extracts from *Ode on the Death of the Duke of Wellington*

I

Bury the Great Duke
With an empire's lamentation,
Let us bury the Great Duke
To the noise of the mourning of a mighty nation,
Mourning when their leaders fall,
Warriors carry the warrior's pall,
And sorrow darkens hamlet and hall.

II

Where shall we lay the man whom we deplore?
Here, in streaming London's central roar.
Let the sound of those he wrought for,
And the feet of those he fought for,
Echo round his bones for evermore.

III

Lead out the pageant: sad and slow,
As fits an universal woe,
Let the long long procession go,
And let the sorrowing crowd about it grow,
And let the mournful martial music blow;
The last great Englishman is low.

IV

Mourn, for to us he seems the last,
Remembering all his greatness in the Past.
No more in soldier fashion will he greet
With lifted hand the gazer in the street.
O friends, our chief state-oracle is mute:
Mourn for the man of long-enduring blood,
The statesman-warrior, moderate, resolute,
Whole in himself, a common good.
Mourn for the man of amplest influence,
Yet clearest of ambitious crime,
Our greatest yet with least pretence,
Great in council and great in war,

Foremost captain of his time,
Rich in saving common-sense,
And, as the greatest only are,
In his simplicity sublime.
O good grey head which all men knew,
O voice from which their omens all men drew,
O iron nerve to true occasion true,
O fall'n at length that tower of strength
Which stood four-square to all the winds that blew!
Such was he whom we deplore.
The long self-sacrifice of life is o'er.
The great World-victor's victor will be seen no more.

V

All is over and done:
Render thanks to the Giver,
England, for thy son.
Let the bell be toll'd.
Render thanks to the Giver,
And render him to the mould.
Under the cross of gold
That shines over city and river,
There he shall rest for ever
Among the wise and the bold.
Let the bell be toll'd:
And a reverent people behold
The towering car, the sable steeds:
Bright let it be with its blazon'd deeds,
Dark in its funeral fold.
Let the bell be toll'd:
And a deeper knell in the heart be knoll'd;
And the sound of the sorrowing anthem roll'd
Thro' the dome of the golden cross;
And the volleying cannon thunder his loss;
He knew their voices of old.

. . . .

VI

Who is he that cometh, like an honour'd guest,
With banner and with music, with soldier and with priest,
With a nation weeping, and breaking on my rest?
Mighty Seaman, this is he
Was great by land as thou by sea.
. . . .
Now, to the roll of muffled drums,
To thee the greatest soldier comes;
For this is he
Was great by land as thou by sea;
His foes were thine; he kept us free;
O give him welcome, this is he
Worthy of our gorgeous rites,
And worthy to be laid by thee;
For this is England's greatest son,
He that gain'd a hundred fights,
Nor ever lost an English gun;
This is he that far away
Against the myriads of Assaye
Clash'd with his fiery few and won;
And underneath another sun,
Warring on a later day,
Round affrighted Lisbon drew
The treble works, the vast designs
Of his labour'd rampart-lines,
Where he greatly stood at bay,
Whence he issued forth anew,
And ever great and greater grew,
Beating from the wasted vines
Back to France her banded swarms,
Back to France with countless blows,
Till o'er the hills her eagles flew
Past the Pyrenean pines,
Follow'd up in valley and glen
With blare of bugle, clamour of men,
Roll of cannon and clash of arms,
And England pouring on her foes.
Such a war had such a close.
Again their ravening eagle rose

In anger, wheel'd on Europe-shadowing wings,
And barking for the thrones of kings;
Till one that sought but Duty's iron crown
On that loud sabbath shook the spoiler down;
A day of onsets of despair!
Dash'd on every rocky square
Their surging charges foam'd themselves away;
Last, the Prussian trumpet blew;
Thro' the long-tormented air
Heaven flash'd a sudden jubilant ray,
And down we swept and charged and overthrew.
So great a soldier taught us there,
What long-enduring hearts could do
In that world's-earthquake, Waterloo!

IX

. . . .
Hush, the Dead March wails in the people's ears:
The dark crowd moves, and there are sobs and tears:
The black earth yawns: the mortal disappears
Ashes to ashes, dust to dust;
He is gone who seem'd so great.—
Gone; but nothing can bereave him
Of the force he made his own
Being here, and we believe him
Something far advanced in State,
And that he wears a truer crown
Than any wreath that man can weave him.
Speak no more of his renown,
Lay your earthly fancies down,
And in the vast cathedral leave him.
God accept him, Christ receive him.

To ask any poet to produce poetry to order is to invite failure and Tennyson, appointed Poet Laureate a year before Wellington died in September 1851, realised that the commemorative poem which would be demanded of him to mark the event represented his first highly important challenge in that office. Fortunately two months elapsed before the ambitious State Funeral could be organised and this allowed Tennyson a decent interval for composition; fortunately, too, he himself was deeply stirred by the death of the Iron Duke and soon found that the theme offered him the unique opportunity to pour into the Ode all his personal admiration for the Duke himself and his heartfelt loyalty to his country and pride in its glorious history. All went well with the work and ten thousand copies of the Ode were on sale in pamphlet form on the day of the funeral. Surprisingly, immediate critical response to the poem was muted while its popularity with the general reading public only gathered slow momentum over the years. However the poem afforded Tennyson himself immediate satisfaction and for the rest of his life it remained one of his favourite poems for reading aloud to visitors at Farringford, his Isle of Wight home. Harold Nicolson in his 1923 biography of Tennyson gives a delightful description of life at Farringford which demands full quotation since it reveals so much about the Tennyson household, the poet himself, and the manner of his poetry readings.

How familiar to us has become the description of the life at Farringford! The regularity and the method of it all; the settled habits becoming, as it were, the etiquette of the house, an etiquette, in later years, almost regal in its rigidity. The honoured but apprehensive guest arriving before sunset in a cab from Yarmouth pier; the momentary glimpse of the poet over the hedge mowing the lawn in spectacles and black sombrero, and hiding, as one approached, behind the juniper; the parlourmaid and the very late Gothic of the drawing-room window; the evening sun upon the cedar outside; the mask of Dante glimmering from the dark red walls and the engraving of Sebastiano del Piambo's Lazarus above the mantelpiece; Mrs Tennyson rising, gentle and nervous, towards one from the sofa, in her grey gown; the anxious, expectant pause; the sense of unbearable imminence—and then, slowly framed in the doorway, the dark bulk of the Laureate. In an awful silence he would advance into the room, a book held close to his, by then, unspectacled eyes. An evanescent introduction from Mrs Tennyson, and those fierce eyes would be turned upon one in a penetrating myopic scrutiny, and a deep growl of acknowledgment, if not of greeting, would proceed from the mass of tangled mane and beard. Another aching pause, and in a crisis of embarrassment one would pass into the dining-room. It was six-thirty by the clock there; how long could all this be possibly expected to last? There was salt beef and carrots and side dishes on the table. The Laureate would begin to carve. A little fluttering conversation about Yarmouth pier from Mrs. Tennyson; a second sudden growl from the Laureate: "I like my meat in wedges," and the subject of Yarmouth pier would flutter down to another prolonged and awful silence. And then gradually, in the appropriate and vacant expectancy thus created, the Laureate would embark with grunt and growl upon some broad Lincolnshire story, a story so broad and so North Country that one would wonder tremulously how much one understood, how much, with Mrs Tennyson there, one could rightly be expected to understand; and with the conclusion would come from the Laureate a loud appropriate guffaw, in contrast to which one's own accordant laughter appeared but a slight and timorous cacchination. Gradually under hammer-blows like this the ice would melt, and with the port a certain geniality, heartening but still very insecure, would descend upon the occasion. But there were worse trials to come. At eight one would be taken to the attic room for a pipe; still apprehensive, one would enter, and from a basket the Laureate would choose a pipe and transfer it, already lighted, to one's own lips. And then there would be a growl or two about some recent review in an obscure periodical; and more stories; and one would sit there in the smoke, wondering why he was so different from what one had expected . . . wondering why he called a novel "a novéll," why he pronounced knowledge with a long *o*, why he gave to the word "too" a thinness of vowel sound which was Cockney rather than Lincolnshire; why he spoke of a pageant as a "paygeant"; why, finally, he sat there, as Mr Gosse has told us, "a gaunt, black, touzled man, rough in speech, brooding like an old gypsy over his inch of clay pipe stuffed with shag and sucking in port wine with gusto."

And then one would descend to the drawing-room, where the curtains had been drawn and the lamps lit; and there was a table in the recessed window, with Mrs Tennyson flickering over the tea-urn and the fruit. And more port. And then the reading would begin.

We have heard a great deal about this reading. It figures prominently in all the endless references to these palpitating visits. He would sometimes read the *Idylls*; more often he would choose the *Ode to the Duke of Wellington*, lengthening the vowels into:

"Bury the greaaat Duke with an empire's lamentaaation."
or
"To the noise of the moourning of a mighty naaation."

Sometimes, and quite incomprehensibly, he would embark upon the *Northern Farmer* and, at other times, he would startle his audience with a very metrical rendering of the *Battle of Brunanburh*. He would never consent to read *In Memoriam*: "I cannot," he said, "it breaks me down so." But it was *Maud* that was his favourite. "Come and let me read you *Maud*," he would say, "you'll never forget it." . . . The eventual comments, when all was over, were facilitated by the fact that Tennyson would generally make them himself. "There's a wonderful touch!" he would say. "That's very tender." All that was expected of the audience during the recitation was their rapt attention, and if, at the end, any comment was exacted, it was easy to evade the point by becoming "broken down." Bayard Taylor (a Farringford visitor who attended one of these recitations) described Tennyson's reading as "a strange, monotonous chant, with unexpected falling inflexions, which I cannot describe, but can imitate exactly."

Fortunately we do in fact possess some practical evidence of Tennyson's manner of reading for in 1890, when he was 80, he was induced by some American emissaries from Thomas Edison to record on a phonograph his renderings of a number of poems which included *Maud*, *The Light Brigade*, *The Northern Farmer* (itself a dialect poem), and the Wellington Ode. The process required the old man to speak into an awkward tube and when some years ago I heard one of these recordings on the radio, for the records are still playable, albeit with much surface interference, I guessed that primitive electronics had lifted the pitch of his voice unnaturally; certainly the timbre was tenor rather than the bass I had expected. But the chant-like effect and the falling inflexions were obvious and these, added to a strong Lincolnshire accent, gave the poems an altogether different "tune" to that derived from one's own silent reading on the page. For example, an Oxford (or BBC?) rendering of:

> Half a league, half a league,
> Half a league onward,
> All in the valley of Death,
> Rode the six hundred

is worlds removed from Tennyson's own mournful chanting which requires syllabic marking and phonetic spelling to convey any conception of his performance:

166

> Haff a laygue, haff a laygue,
> Haff a laygue onwaard,
> All in the valley of Dayth,
> Roade the six hoondrayd,

Or again, listening to the final stanza of *Maud*, one experiences the poem in a totally new way:

> She is coming, my own, my swayte,
> Were it ever so airy a trayde,
> My hairt would hear her and bayte,
> Were it airth in an airthy bayde,
> My doost would hear her and bayte,
> Had I lain for a century dayde,
> Would start and tremble oonder her fayte,
> And blossom in purrple and rayde.

Tennyson, so far as I know, is the only nineteenth-century poet whose voice has been recorded in this fashion: how one would love to have heard Browning and Matthew Arnold! Still more, of course, one longs to have some inkling of the voices and accents of other great poets, Pope, say, or Byron, and as for William Shakespeare . . . !

A Danish scholar has in fact made a study of English pronunciation in Shakespeare's time; by meticulous and painstaking analysis of all the rhymes which Shakespeare ever employed he has established, anyway to his own satisfaction, that English pronunciation in Elizabethan times approximated fairly closely to an Irish accent of to-day. I heard, again on the radio, a recording of a Shakespeare sonnet (No. XVIII) "Shall I compare thee to a summer's day" and very attractive it sounded with the letter *r* being rolled in "summer," "temperate" and "eternal" and the final *g* being dropped in the "darlin' buds of May." But this theory, I fear, is inspired guess-work and I rather doubt if we have any true conception of the "tune" of Shakespearian English in the first Elizabethan age.

I make no apology for this lengthy aside on the reading of poetry for this is an aspect of the art which is too easily ignored. Clearly a poem ultimately stands or falls on its actual content, yet poetry is not intended to be silently lip-read but expressed through

Ayston, Rutland

"Bare ruined choirs where late the sweet birds sang."

W. Shakespeare p.201

the human voice. To an extent the reader of a poem resembles the instrumentalist in music; each can either enhance or impair his material through the technical skill of his performance which, for the poetry reader, must comprise a thorough understanding of the content of the poem, an emotional affinity with its mood, and a combination of clear diction and subtle voice control through the dramatic employment of pace, pause, and pitch. These criteria suggest that poetry requires actors for its interpretation, and it is certainly true that a John Gielguld or a Ralph Richardson can enrich one's appreciation of a poem by their professional renderings. Nevertheless, I believe that the poet himself is often the supreme reader of his own poetry. I think particularly of T. S. Eliot's dry, dead-pan delivery which harmonised perfectly with the conversational, laconic mood of his poetry; of Sir John Betjeman's warm, gentle voice which is equally appropriate to the tender, nostalgic, and melancholy humour of so much of his work; and of the crisp diction and caressing tones of that most gifted of poet/readers, Cecil Day-Lewis. Once one has heard the personal "tune" which the poet himself imparts to his work, the poetry gains an added dimension which contributes powerfully to its unique effect and there can have been few better exemplars of this than Dylan Thomas.

To mention Dylan Thomas is to be reminded yet again of the tendency for so many poets to "chant" their poetry. In this respect we possess one precious piece of firsthand evidence from that vigorous essayist William Hazlitt in his famous description of Coleridge and Wordsworth which comes from his fine essay *My First Acquaintance with Poets*. "The next day," Hazlitt writes:

> Wordsworth arrived from Bristol at Coleridge's cottage (at Nether Stowey). I think I see him now. He answered in some degree to his friend's description of him, but was more gaunt and Don Quixote-like. He was quaintly dressed in a brown fustian jacket and striped pantaloons. There was something of a roll, a lounge in his gait,. . .a severe, worn pressure of thought about his temples, a fire in his eye (as if he saw something in objects more than the outward appearance), an intense high narrow forehead, a Roman nose, cheeks furrowed by strong purpose and feeling, and a convulsive inclination to laughter about the mouth, a good deal at variance with the solemn, stately expression of the rest of the face.. . .He sat down and talked very naturally and freely, with

a mixture of clear gushing accents in his voice, a deep gutteral intonation, and a strong tincture of the northern burr, like the crust on wine. . . There is a 'chaunt' in the recitation both of Coleridge and Wordsworth, which acts as a spell upon the hearer, and disarms the judgment. Perhaps they have deceived themselves by making habitual use of this ambiguous accompaniment. Coleridge's manner is more full, animated, and varied; Wordsworth's more equable, sustained, and internal. The one might be termed more dramatic, the other more lyrical. Coleridge has told me that he himself likes to compose in walking over uneven ground, or breaking through the struggling branches of a copse wood; whereas Wordsworth always wrote (if he could) walking up and down a straight gravel-walk, or in some spot where the continuity of his verse met with no collateral interruption.

Here, then, are four poets—Tennyson, Wordsworth, Coleridge, and Dylan Thomas—who all imparted a chanting tone to their poetry and all employed a variety of regional accents which added a tincture to their readings. Is Hazlitt right? Does such chanting "act as a spell upon the hearer, and disarm the judgment?" Are the poets deceiving *themselves* by this "ambiguous accompaniment?" Perhaps it all comes back to the objective/subjective approach. Too objective a reading may lose something of a poem's emotional depth; too subjective an approach may cloak superficial matter in a vague, emotional blur. As ever, the reader must seek, with Aristotle, the golden mean!

But it is time to return to the battlefield and this time to the field of Holmedon and Harry Percy. In a memorable production in New York in 1946 I was privileged to see Laurence Olivier play Hotspur in Part I of *Henry IV* and, the following evening, Justice Shallow in Part II. Olivier's virility and restlessness on stage were personified in Hotspur where, utilising to the full an aggressive voice and dynamic personality, he created an impetuous and sharp-tempered character who dominated the stage on his every appearance. Olivier also chose to accentuate Hotspur's passionate outbursts by deliberately stammering on the letter *w*. One wondered why he had chosen this particular letter until all was revealed at Hotspur's death, when stretched on the ground, after his fight with the Prince of Wales, he attempts his final speech:

> O! I could prophesy,
> But that the earthy and cold hand of death
> Lies on my tongue. No, Percy, thou art dust,
> And food for w. . . w. . . w. . .

which the Prince obligingly concluded with the appropriate iambic pentameter:

> For worms, brave Percy. Fare thee well, great heart!

The King has accused Hotspur of failing to hand over prisoners captured by him at Holmedon and this is Hotspur's exasperated, but specious, reply:

> My liege, I did deny no prisoners,
> But I remember, when the fight was done,
> When I was dry with rage and extreme toil
> Breathless and faint, leaning upon my sword,
> Came there a certain lord, neat, and trimly drest,
> Fresh as a bridegroom; and his chin new reapt
> Show'd like a stubble-land at harvest-home;
> He was perfumed like a milliner;
> And 'twixt his finger and his thumb he held
> A pouncet-box, which ever and anon
> He gave his nose, and took't away again;—
> Who therewith angry, when it next came there,
> Took it in snuff:—and still he smiled and talked;
> And as the soldiers bore dead bodies by,
> He call'd them untaught knaves, unmannerly,
> To bring a slovenly unhandsome corse
> Betwixt the wind and his nobility.
> With many holiday and lady terms
> He question'd me; amongst the rest, demanded
> My prisoners in your majesty's behalf.
> I then, all smarting with my wounds being cold,
> To be so pestered with a popinjay,
> Out of my grief and my impatience,
> Answer'd neglectingly, I know not what,—
> He should, or he should not; for he made me mad
> To see him shine so brisk, and smell so sweet,
> And talk so like a waiting-gentlewoman
> Of guns and drums and wounds,—God save the mark!—

And telling me the sovereign'st thing on earth
Was parmaceti for an inward bruise;
And that it was great pity, so it was,
This villainous salt-petre should be digg'd
Out of the bowels of the harmless earth,
Which many a good tall fellow had destroy'd
So cowardly; and but for these vile guns,
He would himself have been a soldier.

SIEGFRIED SASSOON
The General

"Good-morning; good morning!" the General said
When we met him last week on our way to the Line.
Now the soldiers he smiled at are most of 'em dead,
And we're cursing his staff for incompetent swine.
"He's a cheery old card," grunted Harry to Jack
As they slogged up to Arras with rifle and pack.

. . . .
But he did for them both by his plan of attack.

WILFRED OWEN
Exposure

Our brains ache, in the merciless iced east winds that knive
    us . . .
Wearied we keep awake because the night is silent . . .
Low, drooping flames confuse our memory of the salient . . .
Worried by silence, sentries whisper, curious, nervous,
    But nothing happens.

Watching, we hear the mad gusts tugging on the wire,
Like twitching agonies of men among its brambles.
Northward, incessantly, the flickering gunnery rumbles,
Far off, like a dull rumour of some other war.
    What are we doing here?

The poignant misery of dawn begins to grow . . .
We only know war lasts, rain soaks, and clouds sag stormy.
Dawn massing in the east her melancholy army
Attacks once more in ranks on shivering ranks of gray,
    But nothing happens.

Sudden successive flights of bullets streak the silence.
Less deathly than the air that shudders black with snow,
With sidelong flowing flakes that flock, pause, and renew;
We watch them wandering up and down the wind's non-
chalance,
But nothing happens.

Pale flakes with fingering stealth come feeling for our
faces—
We cringe in holes, back on forgotten dreams, and stare,
snow-dazed,
Deep into grassier ditches. So we drowse, sun-dozed,
Littered with blossoms trickling where the blackbird fusses.
Is it that we are dying?

Slowly our ghosts drag home: glimpsing the sunk fires,
glozed
With crusted dark-red jewels; crickets jingle there;
For hours the innocent mice rejoice: the house is theirs;
Shelters and doors, all closed; on us the doors are closed,—
We turn back to our dying.

Since we believe not otherwise can kind fires burn;
Nor ever suns smile true on child, or field, or fruit.
For God's invincible spring our love is made afraid;
Therefore, not loath, we lie out here; therefore were born,
For love of God seems dying.

To-night, His frost will fasten on this mud and us,
Shrivelling many hands, puckering foreheads crisp.
The burying-party, picks and shovels in their shaking grasp,
Pause over half-known faces. All their eyes are ice,
But nothing happens.

Some of Owen's poems have, in my opinion, been over-
anthologised to the neglect of some of his finest poems, notably
Exposure. I. M. Parsons, in his selection of 1914–18 poetry, *Men
Who March Away*, rightly calls attention to this poem and to the
outstanding first four stanzas with their wealth of rich metaphor
and imagery which evoke uncannily and intensively the utter
misery of trench warfare. The sudden transition of thought in

the fifth stanza from the snow-filled trenches of Flanders to a sunny hedge in an English spring—the "snow-dazed" soldier dreaming of his "sun-dozed" home—is brilliantly achieved. Thenceforward in the poem the symbols of home and of "God's invincible spring" mingle inextricably with the horrors of winter warfare and lead to the terrible conclusion, "All their eyes are ice."

Owen's mastery of sound effects are worthy of detailed analysis as is his deliberate employment of half-rhymes. This was a feature of all his poetry, and the delicate assonance and consonance which he achieved by these means are perhaps more subtle than the effects of total rhyme.

I. M. Parsons goes on to make an admirable defence of the 1914–18 war poets whose work has been attacked by some critics as too narrowly subjective contained, as it is, within the one over-all experience. Parsons says:

> Pity by now has become almost a dirty word in discussions of First World War poetry. . . . Owen himself, ironically enough, is partly to blame, for the phrase "the poetry is in the pity," which occurs in his brief enigmatic draft *Preface to the Poems*, has been taken from its context to lend support to the view that what these poets were writing about was individual suffering. As such, so the argument runs, their work is narrowly personal, emotionally sub-jective, and devoid of any historical links with the past. It seems to me that the reverse is true: that at any rate the major poems in this book are poems which "look before and after," that have their roots in the mainstream of English poetry. . . in Shakespeare, who wrote of "pity like a naked new-born babe, striding the blast," in Blake and Hopkins, who also understood the meaning of compas-sion (for it is compassion, rather than pity, that informs and inspires them); . . . and you cannot condemn a poem as limitingly subjective just because its origin is tied to a specific event . . . as I see it what the major poets represented there were writing about was not the plight of the individual, still less their own personal plight. They were concerned with something much larger, something which has been the subject of poetry since time immemorial, with:
>
> > . . . Whatever mourns in men
> > Before the last sea and the hapless stars;
> > Whatever mourns when many leave these shores;
> > Whatever shares
> > The eternal reciprocity of tears.

SIEGFRIED SASSOON
The Death-Bed

He drowsed and was aware of silence heaped
Round him, unshaken as the steadfast walls;
Aqueous like floating rays of amber light,
Soaring and quivering in the wings of sleep,
Silence and safety; and his mortal shore
Lipped by the inward moonless waves of death.

Some one was holding water to his mouth.
He swallowed, unresisting; moaned and dropped
Through crimson gloom to darkness; and forgot
The opiate throb and ache that was his wound.
Water—calm, sliding green above the weir;
Water—a sky-lit alley for his boat,
Bird-voiced, and bordered with reflected flowers
And shaken hues of summer; drifting down,
He dipped contented oars, and sighed, and slept.

Night, with a gust of wind, was in the ward,
Blowing the curtain to a glimmering curve.
Night. He was blind; he could not see the stars
Glinting among the wraiths of wandering cloud;
Queer blots of colour, purple, scarlet, green,
Flickered and faded in his drowning eyes.

Rain; he could hear it rustling through the dark;
Fragrance and passionless music woven as one;
Warm rain on drooping roses; pattering showers
That soak the woods: not the harsh rain that sweeps
Behind the thunder, but a trickling peace
Gently and slowly washing life away.

. . . .

He stirred, shifting his body; then the pain
Leaped like a prowling beast, and gripped and tore
His groping dreams with grinding claws and fangs.
But some one was beside him; soon he lay
Shuddering because that evil thing had passed.
And death, who'd stepped toward him, paused and stared.

Light many lamps and gather round his bed.
Lend him your eyes, warm blood, and will to live.
Speak to him; rouse him; you may save him yet.
He's young; he hated war; how should he die
When cruel old campaigners win safe through?

But Death replied: "I choose him." So he went,
And there was silence in the summer night;
Silence and safety; and the veils of sleep.
Then, far away, the thudding of the guns.

A. E. HOUSMAN
Epitaph on an Army of Mercenaries

These, in the day when heaven was falling,
   The hour when earth's foundations fled,
Followed their mercenary calling
   And took their wages and are dead.

Their shoulders held the sky suspended;
   They stood, and earth's foundations stay;
What God abandoned, these defended,
   And saved the sum of things for pay.

WILFRED OWEN
Dulce et Decorum Est

Bent double, like old beggars under sacks,
Knock-kneed, coughing like hags, we cursed through
    sludge,
Till on the haunting flares we turned our backs
And towards our distant rest began to trudge.
Men marched asleep. Many had lost their boots
But limped on, blood-shod. All went lame; all blind;
Drunk with fatigue; deaf even to the hoots
Of tired, outstripped Five-Nines that dropped behind.

Gas! Gas! Quick, boys!—An ecstasy of fumbling,
Fitting the clumsy helmets just in time;
But someone still was yelling out and stumbling
And flound'ring like a man in fire or lime . . .
Dim through the misty panes and thick green light,
As under a green sea, I saw him drowning.

In all my dreams, before my helpless sight,
He plunges at me, guttering, choking, drowning.
If in some smothering dreams you too could pace
Behind the wagon that we flung him in,
And watch the white eyes writhing in his face,
His hanging face, like a devil's sick of sin;
If you could hear, at every jolt, the blood
Come gargling from the froth-corrupted lungs,
Obscene as cancer, bitter as the cud
Of vile, incurable sores on innocent tongues,
My friend, you would not tell with such high zest
To children ardent for some desperate glory,
The old Lie: Dulce et decorum est
Pro patria mori.

In general terms "my" war was poetically unproductive. In some
ways, I suppose, the trauma was no longer novel, nor, after a few
weeks in 1939–40, were the monotony and horror of trench warfare resurrected—the bulk of the 1914–18 war poetry, after all, had
sprung from the soldiers in the trenches. It is a curious fact that in
neither war did the Senior Service or the RAF make a significant
poetic contribution; perhaps they were too busy! But mercifully
the bulk of the 1940–42 army was girding its loins at home and
"battle-skills" were being acquired in Nissen Huts and the Highlands of Scotland rather than under actual shell-fire. So the worst
lesson which the conscripted civilian had to learn was how to
adjust to the rigidities of army thought and practice as exemplified
in War Office training manuals and as executed by Colonel Blimp
and his non-commissioned officers. Henry Reed, in two Lessons of
War poems, *Judging Distances* and *Naming of Parts*, captures with
engaging humour the genuine spirit of the age just as Evelyn
Waugh did in novel form in his *Put Out More Flags*. It is difficult

to exclude either poem, so deliciously does each lampoon army phraseology and attitudes, but I think the NCO with his squad on the Bren Gun in *Naming of Parts* must be first choice; nevertheless, a limited extract from *Judging Distances* positively demands inclusion:

And at least you know
That maps are of time, not place, so far as the army
Happens to be concerned—the reason being,
Is one which need not delay us. Again you know

There are three kinds of tree; three only, the fir and the
    poplar,
And those which have bushy tops to; and lastly
    That things only seem to be things.

A barn is not called a barn, to put it more plainly,
Or a field in the distance, where sheep may be safely grazing.
You must never be over-sure. You must say, when re-
    porting:
At five o'clock in the central sector is a dozen
Of what appear to be animals; whatever you do,
    Don't call the bleeders sheep.

HENRY REED
Naming of Parts

Vixi duellis nuper idoneus
Et militavi non sine gloria

Today we have naming of parts. Yesterday,
We had daily cleaning. And to-morrow morning,
We shall have what to do after firing. But to-day,
To-day we have naming of parts. Japonica
Glistens like coral in all of the neighbouring gardens,
    And to-day we have naming of parts.

This is the lower sling swivel. And this
Is the upper sling swivel, whose use you will see,
When you are given your slings. And this is the piling
    swivel,
Which in your case you have not got. The branches
Hold in the gardens their silent, eloquent gestures,
    Which in our case we have not got.

This is the safety-catch, which is always released
With an easy flick of the thumb. And please do not let me
See anyone using his finger. You can do it quite easy
If you have any strength in your thumb. The blossoms
Are fragile and motionless, never letting anyone see
    Any of them using their finger.

And this you can see is the bolt. The purpose of this
Is to open the breech, as you see. We can slide it
Rapidly backwards and forwards: we call this
Easing the spring. And rapidly backwards and forwards
The early bees are assaulting and fumbling the flowers:
    They call it easing the Spring.

They call it easing the Spring: it is perfectly easy
If you have any strength in your thumb: like the bolt,
And the breech, and the cocking-piece, and the point of
    balance,
Which in our case we have not got; and the almond-blossom
Silent in all of the gardens and the bees going backwards
    and forwards,
    For to-day we have naming of parts.

    This poem clearly needs either two readers or the reader himself
to undertake the contrasting characters. Roughly the first four
lines of each stanza should be spoken in strident, NCO tones in
a London (but not actually cockney) accent; the last lines of each
stanza and the whole of the final stanza are, of course, the ironic
comments of a bourgeois, *New Statesman* type conscript: ideally,
the accent should be Noel Coward!
    I am again indebted to C. B. Cox and A. E. Dyson in their
Practical Criticism of Poetry for an illuminating analysis of the next
poem. But, first, the poem itself.

Ted Hughes
Six Young Men

The celluloid of a photograph holds them well,—
Six young men, familiar to their friends.
Four decades that have faded and ochre-tinged
This photograph have not wrinkled the faces or the hands.
Though their cocked hats are not now fashionable,
Their shoes shine. One imparts an intimate smile,
One chews a grass, one lowers his eyes, bashful,
One is ridiculous with cocky pride—
Six months after this picture they were all dead.

All are trimmed for a Sunday jaunt. I know
That bilberried bank, that thick tree, that black wall,
Which are there yet and not changed. From where these sit
You hear the water of seven streams fall
To the roarer in the bottom, and through all
The leafy valley a rumouring of air go.
Pictured here, their expressions listen yet,
And still that valley has not changed its sound
Though their faces are four decades under the ground.

This one was shot in an attack and lay
Calling in the wire, then this one, his best friend,
Went out to bring him in and was shot too;
And this one, the very moment he was warned
From potting at tin-cans in no-man's land,
Fell back dead with his rifle-sights shot away.
The rest, nobody knows what they came to,
But come to the worst they must have done, and held it
Closer than all their hope; all were killed.

Here see a man's photograph,
The locket of a smile, turned overnight
Into the hospital of his mangled last
Agony and hours; see bundled in it
His mightier-than-a-man dead bulk and weight:
And on this one place which keeps him alive
(In his Sunday best) see fall war's worst
Thinkable flash and rending, onto his smile
Forty years rotting into soil.

That man's not more alive whom you confront
And shake by the hand, see hale, hear speak loud.
Than any of these six celluloid smiles are,
Nor prehistoric or fabulous beast more dead;
No thought so vivid as their smoking blood:
To regard this photograph might well dement,
Such contradictory permanent horrors here
Smile from the single exposure and shoulder out
One's own body from its instant and heat.

Discussion topics

Stanza 1

a. In what way does the word "holds" contain the full emotional force of the poem? What other meaning does it imply apart from the obvious one? Is there a link with the third stanza "and held it closer than all their hope?"

b. In what way does the homely detail of the young men's appearance add to the emotional impact of the poem?

c. Is there any hint before the last line that the six men are dead?

Stanza 2

d. What is the contrast between the place and the men themselves which adds poignancy to the theme?

Stanza 3

e. "The last three lines have a distancing effect which is strangely moving" (Cox and Dyson). Do you agree?

Stanza 4

f. In what ways is the photograph itself a victim of war?

g. Which word in this stanza strikes you with the greatest force? Why?

Stanza 5

h. Is the word "exposure" being used in two senses?

i. Is Hughes saying in this final stanza that the six celluloid dead are, in a sense, more alive than the man-in-the-street today? If so, in what sense is this true?

WILFRED OWEN
Spring Offensive

Halted against the shade of a last hill,
They fed, and, lying easy, were at ease
And, finding comfortable chests and knees,
Carelessly slept. But many there stood still
To face the stark, blank sky beyond the ridge,
Knowing their feet had come to the end of the world.

Marvelling they stood, and watched the long grass swirled
By the May breeze, murmurous with wasp and midge,
For though the summer oozed into their veins
Like an injected drug for their bodies' pains,
Sharp on their souls hung the imminent line of grass,
Fearfully flashed the sky's mysterious glass.

Hour after hour they ponder the warm field—
And the far valley behind, where the buttercup
Had blessed with gold their slow boots coming up,
Where even the little brambles would not yield,
But clutched and clung to them like sorrowing hands;
They breathe like trees unstirred.

Till like a cold gust thrills the little word
At which each body and its soul begird
And tighten them for battle. No alarms
Of bugles, no high flags, no clamorous haste—
Only a lift and flare of eyes that faced
The sun, like a friend with whom their love is done.
O larger shone that smile against the sun,—
Mightier than his whose bounty these have spurned.

So, soon they topped the hill, and raced together
Over an open stretch of herb and heather
Exposed. And instantly the whole sky burned
With fury against them; earth set sudden cups
In thousands for their blood; and the green slope
Chasmed and steepened sheer to infinite space.

. . . .

Of them who running on that last high place
Breasted even the rapture of bullets, or went up
On the hot blast and fury of hell's upsurge,
Or plunged and fell away past this world's verge,
Some say God caught them even before they fell.

But what say such as from existence' brink
Ventured but drave too swift to sink?
The few who rushed in the body to enter hell,
And there out-fiending all its fiends and flames
With superhuman inhumanities,
Long-famous glories, immemorial shames—
And crawling slowly back, have by degrees
Regained cool peaceful air in wonder—
Why speak not they of comrades that went under?

SIEGFRIED SASSOON
Everyone Sang

Everyone suddenly burst out singing;
And I was filled with such delight
As prisoned birds must find in freedom,
Winging wildly across the white
Orchards and dark-green fields; on—on—and out of sight.

Everyone's voice was suddenly lifted;
And beauty came like the setting sun:
My heart was shaken with tears; and horror
Drifted away . . . . O, but Everyone
Was a bird; and the song was wordless; the singing will
    never be done.

THOMAS HARDY
In Time of 'The Breaking of Nations' (1915)

Only a man harrowing clods
    In a slow silent walk
With an old horse that stumbles and nods
    Half asleep as they stalk.

Only thin smoke without flame
    From the heaps of couch-grass;
Yet this will go onward the same
    Though Dynasties pass.

Yonder a maid and her wight
    Come whispering by:
War's annals will cloud into night
    Ere their story die.

X

Seasons

There follows, with minimum commentary, a number of poems linked loosely by the thematic thread of the seasons of the year. Although some two hundred and fifty years separate the writing of the first two poems, each remains equally relevant to our own time and each expresses the poet's theme with perfect economy of expression and mastery of technique. Robert Herrick, a Devonshire parson who remained a complacent bachelor throughout his life, tended by his faithful housekeeper, Prue, and himself training a tame pig to drink beer from a tankard, delighted in giving dedicatory titles to his mellifluous lyrics—"To Mistress Katherine Bradshaw, the lovely, that crowned him with laurel," "To Anthea, who may command him anything," "To Dean Bourn, a rude River in Devon, by which sometimes he lived," but here he writes simply.

ROBERT HERRICK
To Daffodils

Fair daffodils, we weep to see
   You haste away so soon;
As yet the early-rising sun
   Has not attain'd his noon.
      Stay, stay
   Until the hasting day
      Has run
   But to the evensong;
And, having prayed together, we
   Will go with you along.

We have short time to stay, as you,
   We have as short a spring;
As quick a growth to meet decay,
   As you, or anything.

We die,
As your hours do, and dry
Away
Like to the Summer's rain;
Or as the pearls of morning's dew
Ne'er to be found again.

And here is Rudyard Kipling in what is for him an exceptionally quiet and restrained mood:

Cities and Thrones and Powers
Stand in Time's eye,
Almost as long as flowers,
Which daily die:
But, as new buds put forth
To glad new men,
Out of the spent and unconsidered Earth
The Cities rise again.

This season's Daffodil,
She never hears
What change, what chance, what chill,
Cut down last year's;
But with bold countenance,
And knowledge small,
Esteems her seven days' continuance
To be perpetual.

So Time that is o'er kind
To all that be,
Ordains us e'en as blind,
As bold as she;
That in our very death,
And burial sure,
Shadow to shadow, well persuaded, saith,
'See how our works endure!'

In both these poems the rhythm is very dominant. To what extent do the rhythms dictate the mood of the poems?

EDWARD THOMAS
Fifty Faggots

There they stand, on their ends, the fifty faggots
That once were underwood of hazel and ash
In Jenny Pinks's Copse. Now, by the hedge
Close packed, they make a thicket fancy alone
Can creep through with the mouse and wren. Next Spring
A blackbird or a robin will nest there,
Accustomed to them, thinking they will remain
Whatever is for ever to a bird:
This Spring it is too late; the swift has come.
'Twas a hot day for carrying them up:
Better they will never warm me, though they must
Light several Winter's fires. Before they are done
The war will have ended, many other things
Have ended, maybe, that I can no more
Foresee or more control than robin or wren.

It is no surprise to learn that Edward Thomas, before his tragic death in action in World War I, met Robert Frost and came under his influence. The line "whatever is for ever to a bird" is pure Frost and the conversational writing style, where emotion seems to be deliberately underplayed, directly echoes Frost. Thomas, like Hardy, was a true countryman and was also able, like him, to impart a universal significance to rural scenes and events.

EDWARD THOMAS
February Afternoon

Men heard this roar of parleying starlings, saw,
   A thousand years ago even as now,
   Black rooks with white gulls following the plough
So that the first are last until a caw
Commands that last are first again,—a law
   Which was of old when one, like me, dreamed how
   A thousand years might dust lie on his brow
Yet thus would birds do between hedge and shaw.

Time swims before me, making as a day
  A thousand years, while the broad ploughland oak
  Roars mill-like and men strike and bear the stroke
  Of war as ever, audacious or resigned,
And God still sits aloft in the array
  That we have wrought him, stone-deaf and stone-blind.

T. E. HULME
Autumn

A touch of cold in the Autumn night—
  I walked abroad,
And saw the ruddy moon lean over a hedge
Like a red-faced farmer.
I did not stop to speak, but nodded,
And round about were the wistful stars
With white faces like town children.

THOMAS HARDY
Weathers

This is the weather the cuckoo likes,
  And so do I;
When showers betumble the chestnut spikes,
  And nestlings fly;
And the little brown nightingale bills his best,
And they sit outside at "The Traveller's Rest,"
And maids come forth sprig-muslin drest,
And citizens dream of the South and West.
  And so do I.

This is the weather the shepherd shuns,
  And so do I;
When beeches drip in browns and duns,
  And thresh, and ply;
And hill-hid tides throb, throe on throe,
And meadow rivulets overflow,
And drops on gate-bars hang in a row,
And rooks in families homeward go,
  And so do I.

"O for a life of sensations rather than of thoughts" wrote Keats, ". . . the Setting Sun will always set me to rights, or if a Sparrow come before my Window, I take part in its existence and pick about the gravel." W. R. Rodgers' *Stormy Day* attempts this "life of sensations rather than thoughts" through a series of sharp observations shaped into exuberant imagery:

O look how the loops and balloons of bloom
Bobbing on long strings from the finger-ends
And knuckles of the lurching cherry-tree
Heap and hug, elbow and part, this wild day,
Like a careless carillon cavorting;
And the beaded whips of the beeches splay
And dip like anchored weed round a doomed rock,
And hovering effortlessly the rooks
Hang on the wind's effrontery as if
On hooks, then loose their hold and slide away
Like sleet sidewards down the warm swimming sweep
Of wind. O it is a lovely time when
Out of the sunk and rigid sumps of thought
Our hearts rise and race with new sounds and sights
And signs, tingling delightedly at the sting
And crunch of springless carts on gritty roads,
The caught kite dangling in the skinny wires,
The swipe of a swallow across the eyes,
Striped awnings stretched on lawns. New things surprise
And stop us everywhere. In the parks
The fountain's scoop and flower like rockets
Over the oval ponds whose even skin
Is pocked and goosefleshed by their niggling rain
That frocks a naked core of statutary.
And at jetty's jut, roped and ripe for hire,
The yellow boats lie yielding and lolling,
Jilted and jolted like jellies. But look!
There! Do you see, crucified on palings,
Motionless news-posters announcing
That now the frozen armies melt and meet
And smash? Go home now, for, try as you may,
You will not shake off that fact to-day.

Behind you limps that dog with tarry paw,
As behind him, perfectly-timed, follows
The dumb shadow that mimes him all the way.

There is an obvious "volta" of thought in this poem which, it is no surprise to learn, was first published in 1941.

A. E. HOUSMAN
Poem IX (from *Last Poems*)

The chestnut casts his flambeaux, and the flowers
  Stream from the hawthorn on the wind away,
The doors clap to, the pane is blind with showers.
  Pass me the can, lad; there's an end of May.

There's one spoilt spring to scant our mortal lot,
  One season ruined of our little store.
May will be fine next year as like as not:
  Oh ay, but then we shall be twenty-four.

We for a certainty are not the first
  Have sat in taverns while the tempest hurled
Their hopeful plans to emptiness, and cursed
  Whatever brute and blackguard made the world.

It is in truth iniquity on high
  To cheat our sentenced souls of aught they crave,
And mar the merriment as you and I
  Fare on our long fool's-errand to the grave.

Iniquity it is; but pass the can.
  My lad, no pair of kings our mothers bore;
Our only portion is the estate of man:
  We want the moon, but we shall get no more.

If here to-day the cloud of thunder lours
  To-morrow it will hie on far behests;
The flesh will grieve on other bones than ours
  Soon, and the soul will mourn in other breasts.

The troubles of our proud and angry dust
  Are from eternity, and shall not fail.
Bear them we can, and if we can we must.
  Shoulder the sky, my lad, and drink your ale.

Housman's lonely but proud Stoic philosophy was never stated more eloquently than in this final stanza.

RUPERT BROOKE
The Old Vicarage, Grantchester
(Café des Westens, Berlin, May 1912)

Just now the lilac is in bloom,
All before my little room;
And in my flower-beds, I think,
Smile the carnation and the pink;
And down the borders, well I know,
The poppy and the pansy blow . . .
Oh! there the chestnuts, summer through,
Beside the river make for you
A tunnel of green gloom, and sleep
Deeply above; and green and deep
The stream mysterious glides beneath,
Green as a dream and deep as death
—Oh, damn! I know it! and I know
How the May fields all golden show,
And when the day is young and sweet,
Gild gloriously the bare feet
That run to bathe . . .
        Du lieber Gott!

Here am I, sweating, sick, and hot,
And there the shadowed waters fresh
Lean up to embrace the naked flesh.
Temperamentvoll German Jews
Drink beer around;—and *there* the dews
Are soft beneath a moon of gold.
Here tulips bloom as they are told;
Unkempt about those hedges blows
An English unofficial rose;

And there the unregulated sun
Slopes down to rest when day is done,
And wakes a vague unpunctual star,
A slippered Hesper; and there are
Meads towards Haslingfield and Coton
Where *das Betreten's* not *verboten.*
          Eιθε γενοιμην . . . would I were
In Grantchester, in Grantchester!—
Some, it may be, can get in touch
With Nature there, or Earth, or such.
And clever modern men have seen
A Faun a-peeping through the green,
And felt the Classics were not dead,
To glimpse a Naiad's reedy head,
Or hear the Goat-foot piping low: . . .
But these are things I do not know.
I only know that you may lie
Day-long and watch the Cambridge sky,
And, flower-lulled in sleepy grass,
Hear the cool lapse of hours pass,
Until the centuries blend and blur
In Grantchester, in Grantchester . . .
Still in the dawnlit waters cool
His ghostly Lordship swims his pool,
And tries the strokes, essays the tricks,
Long learnt on Hellespont, or Styx.
Dan Chaucer hears his river still
Chatter beneath a phantom mill.
Tennyson notes, with studious eye,
How Cambridge waters hurry by . . .
And in that garden, black and white,
Creep whispers through the grass all night;
And spectral dance, before the dawn,
A hundred Vicars down the lawn;
Curates, long dust, will come and go
On lissom, clerical, printless toe;
And oft between the boughs is seen
The sly shade of a Rural Dean . . .
Till, at a shiver in the skies,
Vanishing with Satanic cries,

The prim ecclesiastic rout
Leaves but a startled sleeper-out,
Grey heavens, the first bird's drowsy calls,
The falling house that never falls.
. . . .
Ah God! to see the branches stir
Across the moon at Grantchester!
To smell the thrilling-sweet and rotten
Unforgettable, unforgotten
River-smell, and hear the breeze
Sobbing in the little trees.
Say, do the elm-clumps greatly stand
Still guardians of that holy land?
The chestnuts shade, in reverend dream,
The yet unacademic stream?
Is dawn a secret shy and cold
Anadyomene, silver-gold?
And sunset still a golden sea
From Haslingfield to Madingley?
And after, ere the night is born,
Do hares come out about the corn?
Oh, is the water sweet and cool,
Gentle and brown, above the pool?
And laughs the immortal river still
Under the mill, under the mill?
Say, is there Beauty yet to find?
And Certainty? and Quiet Kind?
Deep meadows yet, for to forget
The lies, and truths, and pain? . . . oh! yet
Stands the Church clock at ten to three?
And is there honey still for tea?

The appeal of poetry is often highly nostalgic and Rupert
Brooke, pining for England and for his undergraduate days
at Cambridge, certainly wallows in nostalgia as he finds himself
in an alien Berlin shortly before World War I. Sentimental the
poem may be, yet a delicious humour also informs it whilst the
octosyllabic couplet, potentially such a monotonous verse form, is
handled by Brooke with ingenious musical variety.

MATTHEW ARNOLD
Extracts from *Thyrsis*

So, some tempestuous morn in early June,
  When the year's primal burst of bloom is o'er,
    Before the roses and the longest day—
  When garden-walks, and all the grassy floor,
    With blossoms, red and white, of fallen May,
    And chestnut-flowers are strewn—
So have I heard the cuckoo's parting cry,
  From the wet field, through the vext garden-trees,
  Come with the volleying rain and tossing breeze:
The bloom is gone, and with the bloom go I.

Too quick despairer, wherefore wilt thou go?
  Soon will the high Midsummer pomps come on,
    Soon will the musk carnations break and swell,
  Soon shall we have gold-dusted snapdragon,
    Sweet-William with his homely cottage-smell,
    And stocks in fragrant blow;
Roses that down the alleys shine afar,
  And open, jasmine-muffled lattices,
  And groups under the dreaming garden-trees,
And the full moon, and the white evening-star.

Matthew Arnold's first stanza carries echoes of the final stanza
of Keats' *Ode to a Nightingale* when the "immortal bird" ceases its
song and leaves the poet to his solitude:

Adieu! adieu! thy plaintive anthem fades
  Past the near meadows, over the still stream,
    Up the hill-side; and now 'tis buried deep
      In the next valley-glades:
  Was it a vision, or a waking dream?
  Fled is that music:—do I wake or sleep?

PETER YATES
Smelling the End of Green July

Smelling the end of green July
I entered through spiked-gates a London park
To grill my body in the sun,
And to untie thought's parcel of pure dark
Under the blue gaze of the candid sky.

The air was heavy, without breath;
The asphalt paths gave off a hollow ring;
And wearing haloes of shrill birds
The statues watched the flowers withering,
And leaves curl up for Summer's rusty death.

O zoo-like sameness of all parks!
The grasses lick the railings of wrought-iron,
And chairs clink in the shrubbery
As Summer roaring like a shabby lion
Claws at the meaning of the human marks.

I saw the tops of buses wheel
Geranium flashes over pigeon-walls;
And heard the rocket-cries of children
Fly upwards, bursting where the water calls,
And scissors sunlight with a glint of steel.

The wings of slowly dripping light
Pulled boats across a swan-enlightened lake;
And near youth's skipping-ropes of joy
I felt the strings of my old parcel break,
Spilling its cold abstractions with delight.

I watched the games of life begun
Among dead matches, droppings of the birds;
And left thought's parcel on a bench
While I relearned the flight of singing words
Under the blowlamp kisses of the sun.

Discussion topics

A proper appreciation of this poem requires careful examination of the rich imagery and the following questions are intended to point the reader's attention to its principal effects.

a. What metaphor gives a unity of theme to the poem?

b. What contrast is forcefully made in the first stanza?

c. Try to explain the full connotations of the following words as employed in the context of the poem: "spiked," "grill," "rusty," "zoo-like."

d. How does the personification of Summer assist the impact of the third stanza?

e. What dominating emotion does the fourth stanza express?

f. Explain "swan-enlightened lake" and "youth's skipping-ropes of joy."

g. What contrast is pointedly made in the final stanza?

h. Explain the connotation of "blowlamp."

A. E. HOUSMAN
Poem XL (Last Poems)

Tell me not here, it needs not saying,
  What tune the enchantress plays
In aftermaths of soft September
  Or under blanching mays,
For she and I were long acquainted
  And I knew all her ways.

On russet floors, by waters idle,
  The pine lets fall its cone;
The cuckoo shouts all day at nothing
  In leafy dells alone;
And traveller's joy beguiles in autumn
  Hearts that have lost their own.

On acres of the seeded grasses
  The changing burnish heaves;
Or marshalled under moons of harvest
  Stand still all night the sheaves;
Or beeches strip in storms for winter
  And stain the wind with leaves.

Transformation of the old canal: Oakham School's "backs".

"Look thy last on all things lovely
Every hour"

W. de la Mare p.214

Possess, as I possessed a season,
The countries I resign,
Where over elmy plains the highway
Would mount the hills and shine,
And full of shade the pillared forest
Would murmur and be mine.

For nature, heartless, witless nature,
Will neither care nor know
What stranger's feet may find the meadow
And trespass there and go,
Nor ask amid the dews of morning
If they are mine or no.

With the exception of the treatment of Hopkins' *Spring* I have so far made no attempt to analyse a poem in any detail. There are those who are opposed to such a practice anyway; as Wordsworth put it "we murder to dissect." Yet just as no doctor could ever acquire professional knowledge and skill without first performing dissections so the reader of poetry will never advance to any deep appreciation of poetry unless he is prepared to analyse at least some poems in detail in order to develop his initial awareness. For, like any art form, whether it be a painting, a symphony, or a cathedral, our appreciation must necessarily be heightened by understanding something of what the artist or the architect or the composer is attempting to do, something of the materials in which he is working, and something of the fundamental problems governing his particular art form. So, in trying to appreciate a poem, there are certain aspects of the poem which the reader must necessarily examine closely if he is to develop an enlightened understanding of the poem and be able to pass a reasoned judgment upon it.

We have already seen that a poet's raw material is words, and clearly a close examination of his vocabulary, both for its definitive and emotional content, is absolutely vital. Then, the poet's words are structured within a rhythm and a rhyme scheme which also do much to add power and feeling to the words. So the first approach to a poem unquestionably is to give it several readings in order, so far as possible, to understand the poem's general meaning and to tune in, as it were, to the poem's emotional tone. At this stage, with, hopefully, the theme understood at least in outline, it is timely to ask a series of questions. What is the poet's purpose in the poem? What is he trying to express? What is his attitude to his theme? Is his tone cynical, for example, or sentimental, or aggressive, or poignant? If so, why? By what means does he convey his message? What imagery, for example, does he employ? What emotional implications are behind that imagery? To what extent do they enforce the theme? Is the rhythm appropriate to the theme? What of the rhyme-scheme and the general line-structure? Is it possible to perceive what it was that inspired the poet to write in the first place?

By this time the reader, having made several more readings of the whole poem and having given special study to specific phrases or lines, should be in a position to attempt an appreciation of the poem as a whole. And here, one warning. It is vital to tune in to the poet's wave-length! In other words, if you fail to grasp the poet's attitude to his theme you will almost certainly base your critical analysis on a false premise. An appreciation of a poem involves just that—a thorough "appreciation" of what the poet is at least trying to say, even if he doesn't perfectly succeed in saying it, and a true understanding of the poet's rational or emotional attitude to his subject. If these fundamentals are misconstrued, then any critical analysis of any poem must necessarily fail.

Ultimately, having made a close analysis of the poem on the lines of the above suggestions, it is for the reader to attempt a considered judgement on the quality of the poem. Here again, it will help to ask questions; does the poem, for example, add to one's awareness of human existence, or to one's vision of life, or in some way enlarge one's horizons? Does the poem seem true to life and does it give some added significance to its subject? An American critic has described a poem as "offering a kind of genuine insight to the mature reader thereby revealing, however obscurely and elusively, a kind of truth," and it is this insight that the reader should try to establish for himself by approaching the poem with both his rational mind and his emotional sympathies, and so discover his own truth from the poem.

The next poem, heavily anthologised though it is, is an interesting one upon which to attempt a critical analysis because we happen to have Keats' own description as to how it originated and what prompted him to write. Here is an extract from a letter he wrote on Tuesday, 21 September, 1819, from Winchester: "How beautiful the season is now—how fine the air. A temperate sharpness about it. Really, without joking, chaste weather—Dian skies—I never lik'd stubble-fields so much as now—Aye better than the chilly green of the Spring. Somehow a stubble plain looks warm—in the same way that some pictures look warm—This struck me so much in my Sunday's walk that I composed upon it." And three weeks earlier, on 28 August, he had written to his sister, "The delightful Weather we have had for two months is the highest gratification I could receive . . . I should like now to promenade round your Gardens—apple-tasting—pear-tasting—plum-judging—apricot-nibbling—peach-scrunching—Nectarine-sucking and Melon-carving." It is interesting to see how these ideas, having gestated in his mind, are eventually brought to birth in the poem.

JOHN KEATS
Ode to Autumn

Season of mists and mellow fruitfulness,
  Close bosom-friend of the maturing sun;
Conspiring with him how to load and bless
  With fruit the vines that round the thatch-eaves run;
To bend with apples the mossed cottage-trees,
  And fill all fruit with ripeness to the core;
  To swell the gourd, and plump the hazel shells
With a sweet kernel; to set budding more,
And still more, later flowers for the bees,
Until they think warm days will never cease,
  For summer has o'er-brimmed their clammy cells.

Who hath not seen thee oft amid thy store?
  Sometimes whoever seeks abroad may find
Thee sitting careless on a granary floor,
  Thy hair soft-lifted by the winnowing wind;
Or on a half-reaped furrow sound asleep,
  Drowsed with the fume of poppies, while thy hook
  Spares the next swath and all its twinèd flowers;
And sometimes like a gleaner thou dost keep
  Steady thy laden head across a brook;
  Or by a cider-press, with patient look,
    Thou watchest the last oozings, hours by hours.

Where are the songs of Spring? Ay, where are they?
Think not of them, thou hast thy music too,—
While barréd clouds bloom the soft-dying day,
And touch the stubble-plains with rosy hue;
Then in a wailful choir, the small gnats mourn
Among the river sallows, borne aloft
Or sinking as the light wind lives or dies;
And full-grown lambs loud bleat from hilly bourn;
Hedge-crickets sing; and now with treble soft
The redbreast whistles from a garden-croft,
And gathering swallows twitter in the skies.

Keats' remark "Oh for a life of sensations rather than thoughts," has already been quoted and the first stanza, which consists of a whole series of compacted sense-impressions, suitably illustrates his approach to poetry. "Ripeness is all" is the stanza's theme and the vocabulary strongly reinforces this theme: "mellow fruitfulness —maturing—load—bless with fruit—bend with apples—fill with fruit—ripeness to the core—swell the gourd—plump the shells— set budding," the whole culminating in the final two lines:

Until they think warm days will never cease,
For summer hath o'er-brimmed their clammy cells.

Throughout, the sounds echo the sense, the soft *m* and *s* consonants especially pervading the stanza, whilst the vowel sounds are also long and soft . . . core, gourd, more, warm, trees, bees, cease, being particularly effective. Finally the rhythm is rich and languorous, with various lines, through use of enjambement, appearing to meander on indefinitely.

In the second stanza another line of thought intervenes when Keats envisages the Spirit of Autumn "sitting careless on a granary floor" but the richness of the autumnal landscape soon returns with the "fume of poppies," "twinéd flowers," "laden head," and, again, the final two lines culminating in the rich cider-oozings "hours by hours."

If the imagery of the first two stanzas is largely visual, Keats turns to sound-imagery for his third stanza, when, after a final beautiful image of the "barréd clouds" giving "bloom" to the "soft-dying day" and a "rosy hue" to the "stubble-plain" he cites several instances of autumnal sound, the last image of all carrying especially poignant overtones in that only one year after the composition of this poem, during the last autumn of his life, Keats himself would be following the "gathering swallows" to Italy. The sound and rhythmic effects of the third stanza are especially moving, with the open vowel sounds at the end of lines achieving an almost ethereal effect whilst the rhythmic irregularities are beautifully attuned to the light wind rising or falling to the "mourning" of the gnats.

What, then, of the total poetic impact? It is evident that Keats' *Ode to Autumn* enlarges one's apprehension of autumn and enriches one's appreciation of the season for its fructifying abundance. He has succeeded, surely, in "bodying forth" autumn in original fashion and opened our eyes (and ears) to the rich variety of its natural splendours. Rightfully, Keats termed the poem an ode, for the verse in many respects constitutes a sort of autumnal melody harmonising appropriately with the season of fruitful abundance and mellow richness; yet, at the very heart of all this cloying profusion, we hear the first sounds of autumn's approaching dissolution in the twittering of the swallows gathering for their winter flight. Out of the sights and sounds of a normal autumn day, therefore, Keats has created a new and valid emotional experience for his reader and, in the critic's words, revealed "however obscurely and elusively, a kind of truth."

WILLIAM SHAKESPEARE
Sonnet 73

That time of year thou may'st in me behold
When yellow leaves, or none, or few, do hang
Upon those boughs which shake against the cold—
Bare ruined choirs, where late the sweet birds sang.
In me thou seest the twilight of such day
As after sunset fadeth in the west,
Which by-and-by black night doth take away,
Death's second self, that seals up all in rest:
In me thou seest the glowing of such fire
That on the ashes of his youth doth lie,
As the death-bed whereon it must expire,
Consumed with that which it was nourished by.
    This thou perceiv'st, which makes thy love more strong,
    To love that well which thou must leave ere long.

Shakespeare here treats of the autumn of life in three highly compressed metaphors charged with both the rational and emotional processes of change and decay. The concluding couplet, as with so many of Shakespeare's sonnets, appeals, possibly, to "the dark lady" or, again possibly, his patron, the Earl of Southampton, (it's all guesswork) to "make hay while the sun shines." The sonnet in Shakespeare's hands is a wonderfully compacted medium for expressing an eloquent poetic statement—*multum in parvo*.

James Elroy Flecker's chief claim to fame rests on his drama *Hassan* and its hypnotic theme verse of the merchants taking the Golden Road to Samarkand:

> Sweet to ride forth at evening from the wells
>   When shadows pass gigantic on the sand,
> And softly through the silence beat the bells
>   Along the Golden Road to Samarkand.
>
> We travel not for trafficking along:
>   By hotter winds our fiery hearts are fanned:
> For lust of knowing what should not be known
>   We make the Golden Journey to Samarkand.

Here, however, is one of his shorter poems in which he quickly establishes an elegiac mood of sadness and regret for the past.

JAMES ELROY FLECKER
November Eves

> November evenings! Damp and still
> They used to cloak Leckhampton Hill,
> And lie down close on the grey plain,
> And dim the dripping window-pane,
> And send queer winds like Harlequins
> That seized our elms for violins
> And struck a note so sharp and low
> Even a child could feel the woe.

Now fire chased shadow round the room;
Table and chairs grew vast in gloom:
We crept about like mice, while Nurse,
Sat mending, solemn as a hearse,
And even our unlearned eyes
Half closed with choking memories.

Is it the mist or the dead leaves,
Or the dead men—November eves?

"It is the function of poetry," it has been said, "to harmonise
the sadness of the world," and *November Eves* offers a good
illustration of this view.

WALTER DE LA MARE
The Holly

The sturdiest of forest-trees
With acorns is inset;
Wan white blossoms the elder brings
To fruit as black as jet;
But O, in all green English woods
Is aught so fair to view
As the sleek, sharp, dark-leaved holly-tree
And its berries burning through?

Towers the ash; and dazzling green
The larch her tassels wears;
Wondrous sweet are the clots of may
The tangled hawthorn bears;
But O, in heath or meadow or wold
Springs aught beneath the blue
As brisk and trim as a holly-tree bole
With its berries burning through?

When hither, thither, falls the snow,
And blazes small the frost,
Naked amid the winter stars
The elm's vast boughs are tossed;
But O, of all that summer showed
What now to winter's true
As the prickle-beribbed dark holly tree,
With its berries burning through!

Part of Shakespeare's genius lay in his universal awareness of the world about him, animate or inanimate, and his choice of concrete homely detail to bring his observations into sharp focus. Here he portrays winter in remarkably wide-ranging fashion, not only setting that season vividly before us but also giving us a fascinating glimpse into the Elizabethan rural scene.

> When icicles hang by the wall
>   And Dick the shepherd blows his nail,
> And Tom bears logs into the hall,
>   And milk comes frozen home in pail;
> When blood is nipt, and ways be foul,
> Then nightly sings the staring owl
>   Tu-whoo!
> To-whit, Tu-whoo! A merry note!
> While greasy Joan doth keel the pot.
>
> When all about the wind doth blow,
>   And coughing drowns the parson's saw,
> And birds sit brooding in the snow,
>   And Marian's nose looks red and raw;
> When roasted crabs hiss in the bowl—
> Then nightly sings the staring owl
>   Tu-whoo!
> Tu-whit, Tu-whoo! A merry note!
> While greasy Joan doth keel the pot.

EDWARD THOMAS
The Owl

Downhill I came, hungry, and yet not starved;
Cold, yet had heat within me, that was proof
Against the North wind; tired, yet so that rest
Had seemed the sweetest thing under a roof.

Then at the inn I had food, fire, and rest,
Knowing how hungry, cold, and tired was I.
All of the night was quite barred out except
An owl's cry, a most melancholy cry.

Shaken out long and clear upon the hill,
No merry note, nor cause of merriment,
But one telling me plain what I had escaped
And others could not, that night, as in I went.

And salted was my food, and my repose,
Salted and sobered, too, by the bird's voice
Speaking for all who lay under the stars,
Soldiers and poor, unable to rejoice.

To what extent do these last two poems illustrate the distinction between subjective and objective writing? Can you determine the "point of departure" of each of these poems, the spark that ignited the poet's imagination? If Shakespeare's poem is a *generalised* picture of winter, how is it that the poem is composed of specific instances of that season?

XI

CONCLUSIONS

So, we'll go no more a-roving
　　So late into the night,
Though the heart be still as loving,
　　And the moon be still as bright.

For the sword outwears its sheath,
　　And the soul wears out the breast,
And the heart must pause to breathe,
　　And love itself have rest.

Though the night was made for loving,
　　And the day returns too soon,
Yet we'll go no more a-roving
　　By the light of the moon.

Or, as Falstaff put it to Justice Shallow in one of the most haunting lines of Shakespeare,
"We have heard the chimes at mid-night, Master Shallow."

William Shakespeare
Dirge for Fidele

Fear no more the heat o' the sun,
　　Nor the furious winter's rages;
Thou thy worldly task hast done,
　　Home art gone, and ta'en thy wages.
Golden lads and girls all must,
As chimney-sweepers, come to dust.

Fear no more the frown o' the great,
　　Thou art past the tyrant's stroke;
Care no more to clothe and eat,
　　To thee the reed is as the oak.
The sceptre, learning, physic, must
All follow this, and come to dust.

Fear no more the lightning-flash,
  Nor the all-dreaded thunder-stone;
Fear not slander, censure rash;
  Thou hast finished joy and moan.
All lovers young, all lovers must
Consign to thee, and come to dust.

No exerciser harm thee!
Nor no witchcraft charm thee!
Ghost unlaid forbear thee!
Nothing ill come near thee!
Quiet consummation have,
And renownéd be thy grave!

FRANCIS BEAUMONT (?)
Extracts from *On the Tombs in Westminster Abbey*

Mortality, behold, and fear,
What a change of flesh is here!
Think how many royal bones
Sleep within this heap of stones,
Hence removed from beds of ease,
Dainty fare, and what might please,
Fretted roofs, and costly shows,
To a roof that flats the nose:
. . . .
Here's an acre sown indeed
With the richest royalest seed,
That the earth did e'er suck in
Since the first man died for sin.
Here the bones of birth have cried,
'Though Gods they were, as men they died.'
. . . .
Here's a world of pomp and state,
Forgotten, dead, disconsolate;
Think, then, this scythe that mows down kings
Exempts no meaner mortal things.
Then bid the wanton lady tread
Amid these mazes of the dead;

And these truly understood
More shall cool and quench the blood
Than her many sports a day,
And her nightly wanton play.
Bid her paint till day of doom,
To this favour she must come,
Bid the merchant gather wealth
The usurer exact by stealth,
The proud man beat it from his thought,
Yet to this shape all must be brought.

This abrasive poem, first printed in 1619, is commonly attributed to Francis Beaumont, the other half of the famous Beaumont and Fletcher dramatist team of that era, although there are doubts about whether he was in fact the author. Be that as it may, this poem speaks for itself as a powerful utterance which seems to me to gain much of its effect from the juxtapositioning of generalised statements with down-to-earth brutality of expression. As an example, the idea of the death to which even the greatest in the land will eventually succumb is translated directly into flesh and bones mouldering in a "heap of stones" whilst "dainty fare, and what might please" ends ignominiously beneath a "roof that flats the nose." The sardonic humour levelled at the "wanton lady" reminds me of a present-day dramatist, John Osborne, and the Jimmy Porter diatribes of *Look Back in Anger*. Rhythmically, the handling of the octosyllabic couplet is masterly and this is the more remarkable in that the poem achieves its most dramatic moments with several lines of heavy monosyllabic words culminating in the sinister climax "Yet to this shape all must be brought." The vocabulary has a Saxon ring about it reminiscent of Churchill's "blood, toil, tears, and sweat," and numerous powerful verbs—flats, cool, quench, suck, eat—leave us in no doubt of Death's pulverising finality.

After this remorseless poem it is a relief to return to the benevolent Devon vicar, Robert Herrick. In point of fact his message in the first poem (delivered with such delicate subtlety) is no different from Beaumont's, but I hope that Dianeme was sufficiently intelligent to act upon it.

ROBERT HERRICK
To Dianeme

Sweet, be not proud of those two eyes
Which, starlike, sparkle in their skies;
Nor be you proud that you can see
All hearts your captives, yours yet free;
Be you not proud of that rich hair
Which wantons with the love-sick air;
Whereas that ruby which you wear,
Sunk from the tip of your soft ear,
Will last to be a precious stone
When all your world of beauty's gone.

ROBERT HERRICK
His Poetry his Pillar

Only a little more
    I have to write,
    Then I'll give o'er,
And bid the world good-night.

'Tis but a flying minute
    That I must stay,
    Or linger in it;
And then I must away.

O time that cut'st down all
    And scarce leav'st here
    Memorial
Of any men that were.

How many lie forgot
    In vaults beneath?
    And piecemeal rot
Without a fame in death?

Behold this living stone
    I rear for me,
    Ne'er to be thrown
Down, envious Time, by thee.

Pillars let some set up
If so they please:
Here is my hope
And my Pyramides.

G. M. Hopkins
Felix Randal

Felix Randal the farrier, O he is dead then? my duty all
    ended,
Who have watched his mould of man, big-boned and
    hardy-handsome
Pining, pining, till time when reason rambled in it and some
Fatal four disorders, flesh'd there, all contended?

Sickness broke him. Impatient he cursed at first, but
    mended
Being anointed and all; though a heavenlier heart began
    some
Months earlier, since I had our sweet reprieve and ransom
Tender'd to him. Ah well, God rest him all road ever he
    offended!

This seeing the sick endears them to us, us too it endears.
My tongue had taught thee comfort, touch had quench'd
    thy tears,
Thy tears that touch'd my heart, child, Felix, poor Felix
    Randal;

How far from then forethought of, all thy more boisterous
    years,
When thou at the random grim forge, powerful amidst peers,
Didst fettle for the great grey drayhorse his bright and
    battering sandal!

Hopkins' duties as a Jesuit priest took him to Liverpool and he
employs several Lancashire dialect expressions in this sonnet—
"and all," "all road ever" i.e., in whatever way, and "fettle" i.e., put
in order. "Random" has two possible meanings in the context: the
architectural term means "built of stones of irregular shapes and

sizes" but I think that Hopkins may also be applying the term
to the intermittent sounds produced by the blacksmith's blows at
his work.

This poem seems to me a remarkable tour de force in that within
the restricted sonnet space Hopkins succeeds in vividly conveying
the two extremes of Felix Randal, on the one hand, a "big-boned,"
boisterous" man, "powerful amidst peers" and, on the other,
a broken man, "pining, pining" as a sick child in his final fatal
illness.

WALTER DE LA MARE
Fare Well

When I lie where shades of darkness
Shall no more assail mine eyes,
Nor the rain make lamentation
    When the wind sighs;
How will fare the world whose wonder
Was the very proof of me?
Memory fades, must the remembered
    Perishing be?

Oh, when this my dust surrenders
Hand, foot, lip to dust again,
May these loved and loving faces
    Please other men!
May the rusting harvest hedgerow
Still the Traveller's Joy entwine,
And as happy children gather
    Posies once mine.

Look thy last on all things lovely,
Every hour. Let no night
Seal thy sense in deathly slumber
    Till to delight
Thou have paid thy utmost blessing;
Since that all things thou wouldst praise
Beauty took from those who loved them
    In other days.

WILLIAM SHAKESPEARE
From *Measure for Measure*
(Act III, Scene i)

Ay, but to die, and go we know not where;
To lie in cold obstruction, and to rot;
This sensible warm motion to become
A kneaded clod; and the delighted spirit
To bathe in fiery floods, or to reside
In thrilling region of thick-ribbed ice;
To be imprison'd in the viewless winds,
And blown with restless violence round about
The pendant world; or to be worse than worst
Of those that lawless and incertain thoughts
Imagine howling!—'tis too horrible!
The weariest and most loathed worldly life
That ache, age, penury and imprisonment
Can lay on nature, is a paradise
To what we fear of death.

ROBERT BROWNING
Prospice

Fear death?—to feel the fog in my throat,
    The mist in my face,
When the snows begin, and the blasts denote
    I am nearing the place,
The power of the night, the press of the storm,
    The post of the foe;
Where he stands, the Arch Fear in a visible form,
    Yet the strong man must go:
For the journey is done and the summit attained,
    And the barriers fall,
Though a battle's to fight ere the guerdon be gained,
    The reward of it all.
I was ever a fighter, so—one fight more,
    The best and the last!
I would hate that death bandaged my eyes, and forbore,
    And bade me creep past.

No! let me taste the whole of it, fare like my peers
    The heroes of old,
Bear the brunt, in a minute pay glad life's arrears
    Of pain, darkness and cold.
For sudden the worst turns the best to the brave,
    The black minute's at end,
And the elements' rage, the fiend-voices that rave,
    Shall dwindle, shall blend,
Shall change, shall become first a peace out of pain,
    Then a light, then thy breast,
O thou soul of my soul! I shall clasp thee again,
    And with God be the rest!

W. E. Henley, a minor Victorian poet, produced two short poems which both seem to me deserving of the same praise which Dr Johnson gave Gray's *Elegy* and which I have already quoted: "Images which find a mirror in every mind, and sentiments to which every bosom returns an echo."

Invictus, the first poem, naturally follows Browning's *Prospice*: both Henley and Browning display a welcome relish for taking all and everything which the world may throw at them and, in so doing, speak eloquently for the ultimate dignity of man. They reflect the same inherent courage which Dr Johnson maintained on his death-bed: "I will be conquered; I will not capitulate."

W. E. HENLEY
Invictus

Out of the night that covers me,
    Black as the pit from pole to pole,
I thank whatever gods may be
    For my unconquerable soul.

In the fell clutch of circumstance
    I have not winced nor cried aloud.
Under the bludgeonings of chance
    My head is bloody, but unbowed.

Beyond this place of wrath and tears
    Looms but the Horror of the shade,
And yet the menace of the years
    Finds, and shall find, me unafraid.

It matters not how strait the gate,
How charged with punishments the scroll,
I am the master of my fate:
I am the captain of my soul.

Here is W. E. Henley's second "poem of departure." It is reminiscent of Tennyson's:

Sunset and evening star,
And one clear call for me!
And may there be no moaning of the bar,
When I put out to sea.

But I prefer Henley's poem in that it does not seem to strike so conscious an attitude.

W. E. HENLEY
Margaritae Sorori, I.M.

A late lark twitters from the quiet skies;
And from the west,
Where the sun, his day's work ended,
Lingers as in content
There falls on the old, gray city
An influence luminous and serene,
A shining peace.

The smoke ascends
In a rosy-and-golden haze. The spires
Shine, and are changed. In the valley
Shadows rise. The lark sings on. The sun,
Closing his benediction,
Sinks, and the darkening air
Thrills with a sense of the triumphing night—
Night with her train of stars
And her great gift of sleep.

So be my passing!
My task accomplished and the long day done,
My wages taken, and in my heart
Some late lark singing,
Let me be gathered to the quiet west,
The sundown splendid and serene,
Death.

ROBERT LOUIS STEVENSON
Requiem

Under the wide and starry sky,
Dig the grave and let me lie.
Glad did I live and gladly die,
　　And I laid me down with a will.

This be the verse you grave for me:
Here he lies where he longed to be;
Home is the sailor, home from sea,
　　And the hunter home from the hill.

A. E. HOUSMAN
XLVIII (More Poems)
Parta Quies

Good-night; ensured release,
Imperishable peace,
　　Have these for yours,
While sea abides, and land,
And earth's foundations stand,
　　And heaven endures.

When earth's foundations flee,
Nor sky nor land nor sea
　　At all is found,
Content you, let them burn;
It is not your concern;
　　Sleep on, sleep sound.

Thomas Hardy
He Never Expected Much or
A Consideration on His Eighty-sixth Birthday

Well, World, you have kept faith with me,
    Kept faith with me;
Upon the whole you have proved to be
    Much as you said you were.
Since as a child I used to lie
Upon the leaze and watch the sky,
Never, I own, expected I
    That life would all be fair.

'Twas then you said, and since have said,
    Times since have said,
In that mysterious voice you shed
    From clouds and hills around:
'Many have loved me desperately,
Many with smooth serenity,
While some have shown contempt of me
    Till they dropped underground.

'I do not promise overmuch,
    Child; overmuch;
Just neutral-tinted haps and such,'
    You said to minds like mine.
Wise warning for your credit's sake!
Which I for one failed not to take,
And hence could stem such strain and ache
    As each year might assign.

BEN JONSON
From an Ode

It is not growing like a tree
In bulk, doth make man better be;
Or standing long an oak, three hundred year,
To fall a log at last, dry, bald, and sere:
  A lily of a day
  Is fairer far in May,
  Although it fall and die that night—
  It was the plant and flower of light.
In small proportions we just beauties see;
And in short measures life may perfect be.

GLOSSARY OF TERMS

RHYTHM

• The basic rhythmic pulse of English poetry is **iambic**—an unstressed syllable followed by a stressed, e.g.,

> We tra/vel not / for traf/ficking / alone;
>   By hot/ter winds / our fie/ry hearts / are fanned:
> For lust / of know/ing what / should not / be known
>   We take / the Gol/den Road / to Sa/markand.

• A large proportion of English poetry, including all Shakespearian drama, is in **iambic pentameters**, that is five iambic stressed beats to each line,

> A horse, / a horse, / my king/dom for / a horse!

• Where the iambic pentameters are unrhymed the poetry is termed **blank verse**.
• A **trochaic** line is the reverse of the **iambic** with the stressed beat followed by an unstressed:

> Lord, thy / word a/bideth
> And our / footsteps / guideth:
> Who its / truth be/lieveth
> Light and / joy re/ceiveth.

• **Iambic** and **trochaic** "feet" are called **duple** time, whilst the other two types of feet are termed **triple** time. These are **anapaests** (˘˘–) or **dactyls** (–˘˘) e.g.,
Anapaestic:

> He had for/ty-two bo/xes all care/fully packed,
>   With his name / painted clear/ly on each;

Dactylic:

> Fórty yĕars / ŏn, whĕn ă/făr ănd ă/sŭnder
> Pártĕd ăre / thŏse whŏ ăre / sínging tŏ-/dăy.

Of course, poetry often employs a mixture of these feet but essentially the basic pulse in all poetry rests on these four types of beat.
  • *Octosyllabic couplet*
Four-beat rhyming iambic couplets,

> Of manners gentle, of affections mild;
> In wit, a man; simplicity, a child.

TECHNICAL TERMS
  • **Alliteration**—words beginning with the same letter ("alliterations's artful aid"!) e.g.,

> An Austrian army, awfully arrayed,
> Boldly by battery besieged Belgrade, etc.

  • **Consonance**—same-sounding consonants in addition to alliteration, e.g.,

> With throats unslaked, with black lips baked,
> We could not laugh nor wail;
> Through utter drought all dumb we stood!
> I bit my arm, I sucked the blood,
> And cried: A sail! a sail!

Here Coleridge gives an intense impression of thirst by the mixture of *th*, *k* and *l* sounds (aided also by the ugly long *a* vowel sound). Notice that it is the *sound* which matters, e.g., a hard *c* and a *k* are identical.
  • **Assonance**—same-sounding syllables in addition to rhyme, e.g.,

> The very deep did rot: O Christ!
> That ever this should be!
> Yea, slimy things did crawl with legs
> Upon the slimy sea.

Here the repetition of the long *i* vowel sound achieves a horrible effect.

• **Enjambement**—where a line runs over, without punctuation, into the next,

> Earth has not anything to show more fair:
> Dull would he be of soul who could pass by
> A sight so touching in its majesty.

• **End-stopped**—where the line is abruptly and neatly completed by the punctuation,

> A little learning is a dangerous thing;
> Drink deep, or taste not the Pierian spring.

• **Caesura**—a heavy pause in the line,

> Avoid Extremes; × and shun the fault of such
> Who still are pleased too little or too much.
> At every trifle scorn to take offence:
> That always shows great pride, × or little sense;
> Those heads, as stomachs, are not sure the best
> Which nauseate all, × and nothing can digest.
> Yet let not each gay Turn thy rapture move,
> For fools admire, × but men of sense approve.

There is a strong pause-break in the four marked lines where the first half of the line waits, as it were, for the balancing statement of the second half.

• **Bathos**—sudden descent from the sublime to the ridiculous.

• **Paradox**—apparent contradiction which, on closer analysis, can be seen to contain a truth, e.g., "Nothing is capable of being taught," or "The golden rule is that there are no golden rules."

INDEX

The following authors are represented by poems or extracts:

226